A Song of Social Significance

MEMOIRS OF AN ACTIVIST

by Dorothy Epstein

with the editorial assistance of Henry Foner
and with an introduction by Ruby Dee

Ben Yehuda Press

A SONG OF SOCIAL SIGNIFICANCE: Memoirs of an Activist
©2007 Dorothy Epstein. All rights reserved.

Published by Ben Yehuda Press
430 Kensington Road
Teaneck, NJ 07666
http://www.BenYehudaPress.com

For permission to reprint, including distribution of the material in this book as part of a synagogue or school newsletter, please contact: Permissions, Ben Yehuda Press, 430 Kensington Road, Teaneck, NJ 07666. permissions@BenYehudaPress.com.

Ben Yehuda Press books may be purchased for educational, business or sales promotional use. For information, please contact: Special Markets, Ben Yehuda Press, 430 Kensington Road, Teaneck, NJ 07666. markets@BenYehudaPress.com.

Cover photograph ©Therese Mitchell, 1935

Library of Congress Cataloging-in-Publication Data

Epstein, Dorothy, 1913-2006.
    A song of social significance : memoirs of an activist / by Dorothy Epstein ; with the editorial assistance of Henry Foner ; and with an introduction by Ruby Dee. — 1st ed.
        p. cm.
    ISBN-13: 978-0-9769862-9-4 (cloth)
    ISBN-13: 978-0-9769862-7-0 (pbk.)
    1. Epstein, Dorothy, 1913-2006. 2. Labor leaders—United States—Biography. 3. Women political activists—United States—Biography. 4. Businesswomen—United States—Biography. I. Foner, Henry. II. Title.
    HD6509.E67A3 2007
    331.88092--dc22
    [B]

                                        2007017477

1st edition   07 08 09 / 10 9 8 7 6 5 4 3 2 1

Dedicated to Mama, Papa, Bob and Marilyn

Sing me of wars, sing me of breadlines,
Tell me of front page news,
Sing me of strikes and last minute headlines,
Dress your observations in syncopation.

Sing me a song with social significance,
There's nothing else that will do.
It must get hot with what is what,
Or I won't love you.

—Harold Rome, "Sing Me A Song With Social Significance"
from *Pins and Needles*, 1937

Preface

By Henry Foner

(Note: This was written four months
before Dorothy Epstein's death in May, 2006)

The June 14, 1996, issue of the Public Employee Press, official
publication of District Council 37 of the American Federation
of State, County and Municipal Employees (AFL-CIO), contained a special supplement called "AFSCME's Untold Story"
written by editor Bill Schleicher. It began:

> "In the depths of the Great Depression, an unemployed
> teacher named Dorothy Epstein got work in the city
> relief bureau and discovered her true calling as an orga-
> nizer. Millions of working men and women found hope
> and strength in those bleak times by joining unions in the
> country's greatest labor upsurge."

It was no accident that Schleicher selected Dorothy Epstein to
typify the dramatic struggles of the welfare workers who fought
side by side with the throngs of unemployed to achieve "a more
humane welfare system, civil service rights and racial justice."
For, as Schleicher pointed out, "Dorothy Epstein never stopped
organizing." This memoir is the account of a career, still current,

HENRY FONER is currently co-historian of the Labor Arts website
(www.laborarts.org). He also co-edits the newsletter of the New
York Labor History Association, "Work History News," and is
a member of the editorial board of *Jewish Currents* magazine. He
formerly served as president of the Fur and Leather Workers Union
from 1961 until his retirement in 1988. He has taught classes in
labor history at the Harry Van Arsdale School for Labor Studies,
the City College Center for Worker Education and the Institute
for Retirees Pursuing Education (IRPE) at Brooklyn College.

that has already spanned over 70 years and that covers the most significant events of a century replete with such happenings. In truth, Dorothy Epstein's story is "a song of social significance" and gives living meaning to Harold Rome's famous song from the show, "Pins and Needles." Whatever the events of that important period—whether the story of an immigrant family in the southeast Bronx section of New York City that struggled to make this a real "golden land," or Dorothy's organization of her fellow workers in New York City's Welfare Department, or her work in the congressional campaigns of Vito Marcantonio, a genuine "people's Congressman," or her creative contributions to the colorful bazaars of the American Jewish Labor Council, or her management of probably the first trade union dental clinic, or her participation in the dramatic "vitamin story" that has played so important a role in our ongoing effort to improve our nation's health, or her inspiring efforts, as a Hunter College graduate, to repay that institution for providing her with a free college education, or, most recently, her role in mobilizing and training senior citizens to help shape a more equitable society, in fact, wherever one turns to examine the events of that remarkable 20th Century, one finds the fine hand and keen organizational skill of Dorothy Epstein.

This memoir is indeed the story of a life of social significance, still unfinished. One is reminded of Carl Sandburg's account in "The People, Yes," of a visitor's conversation with a rural area native. "Lived here all your life?" asks the visitor. "Not yet," is the native's terse but meaningful reply.

In similar manner, Dorothy Epstein, at 92, has not only not yet lived all her life, but is adding to its luster and meaning with each passing day and week. I am proud to have had a hand in bringing that story to readers of every age who have so much to learn from it.

Introduction

By Ruby Dee

In one of the many coincidences that have dotted my life, I wrote this introduction to Dorothy Epstein's fascinating memoir just after Ossie and I were told that we would be receiving the much coveted John F. Kennedy Center's Lifetime Achievement Award. I call it a coincidence because, in the course of her varied and productive life, Dorothy has received more awards than I can remember, much less enumerate. What is most remarkable is that all of them have come after she retired from her "job" and all have been in recognition of her contributions to the community she inhabits and the college from which she graduated–Hunter College in New York City.

And thereby hangs still another coincidence, for I, too, am a Hunter alumna and although I entered a full ten years after she did, I share Dorothy's deep sense of gratitude for the education, free from tuition's tolls, with which Hunter provided us.

The literature courses I took there gave me a greater appreciation of both the written and spoken word and my entire college career served to increase my capacity to absorb the richness of the human experience.

Dorothy and I share two other distinctions resulting from our college years. We have both been inducted into the Hunter College Hall of Fame and we have both received special alumni awards—mine for outstanding professional achievement and hers for distinguished community service.

RUBY DEE is an actor, poet, playwright, screenwriter, journalist and activist. She grew up in Cleveland and was raised in Harlem, New York. She graduated from Hunter College in 1945. Her name and that of her late husband, actor Ossie Davis, have always been associated with struggles for civil rights.

Dorothy's career illustrates another belief we have in common, and that is in the importance of remaining active and involved in the causes we hold dear. My devotion to this theme is so much a part of my life that I hardly have to think about it. Dorothy's takes the form of an ongoing determination to make the lives of senior citizens more meaningful and rewarding. Abraham Lincoln once said that God must love the common people, since he made so many of them. In the age in which we live, the same can be said about our senior population, and Dorothy's creative idea of launching the Institute for Senior Action has created a ripple effect that has spread far and wide, engulfing community organizations and trade unions alike.

There is almost a poetic justice in the fact that the source of Dorothy's livelihood lay in making life-strengthening vitamins available to a more health-conscious nation. In a sense, her activities since her so-called retirement have been equally enhancing to the lives of her contemporaries. I am happy to provide this tribute to a fruitful life and proud to call the person who has lived it my sister.

Foreword
By Dorothy Epstein

This is my first book. In the course of a long and still active life, I have had many occasions to use my writing skills as
an organization tool—for carefully prepared speeches, for articles in union and trade publications, for leaflets, petitions and
testimony at hearing—especially for leaflets. Political activists
of my generation know only too well the important role that
leaflets play in those activities. In fact, there were times when I
could not pass a mimeograph machine without experiencing an
empathetic tug at my heartstrings.

Before that, during my years at school, my essays were creative exercises. My job as senior editor in high school taught
me the skills of writing and editing. Much of my work won
praise—"That was told clearly"—"My, that was a good speech"
—but no one suggested that I write a novel, or even a short
story, and I had no urge to do so.

But none of those writing assignments were comparable to the
decision to reconstruct this story of my life. And yet the variety
of experiences that I have been privileged to undergo—growing
up in a close-knit immigrant family that faced more than its
share of hardships, enjoying the advantages of a long-vanished
tuition-free higher education, playing a role in the most dramatic upsurge of our country's labor movement in its history,
interacting with some of the most exciting political figures that
have graced our public scene, having an opportunity to assist in
the development of a major contribution to public health, and,
most recently, fashioning an innovative program that enables
our growing senior population to continue to live fruitful lives
—all of these have served to persuade me that I do have a story
worth telling.

To take just one example, so few people today know firsthand about the remarkable upsurge of the labor movement dur-

ing the crisis-ridden 1930s and '40s. At the height of this trade union explosion, 35 million working men and women—black and white, native and foreign-born, in every part of the country—were in unions, achieving wages and working conditions that were the envy of the rest of the world. Today, when the labor movement is literally fighting for its life and working families' living standards have slipped downward, it is important to recall the lessons of unity and solidarity that were the hallmarks of that period of growth.

And so, at the age of 92, with the pace of my activities somewhat slowed, I have decided to respond positively to the urgings of so many of my friends and colleagues to finally "put it down on paper." I hope that this book will help convey to its readers the value of the indispensable trait of tenacity which is the backbone of successful activity. I particularly hope that my story will help kindle the flames of activism among present and budding seniors. May it also provide a measure of inspiration to our enthusiastic and dedicated young people who face formidable challenges in the ongoing struggle to achieve a more equitable and peaceful society.

Acknowledgments

This work has traversed a circuitous route in achieving its treasured goal of publication. It began when Bill Schleicher, editor of the *Public Employee Press*, published by District Council 37 of the American Federation of State, County and Municipal Employees (AFSCME), included a special four-page supplement in the newspaper's June 14, 1996, issue celebrating AFSCME's 60th anniversary. Bill made me the central figure in the fascinating contextual account of the union's conception and growth, which he told me he had been preparing for months. After its highly acclaimed appearance, which earned the paper first prizes from the International Labor Press Association for both its text and graphics, Bill urged me to expand the account into a full-sized memoir and offered his assistance in preparing it. Many of my friends echoed his sentiments, but at that time, I just wasn't ready.

Over the next few years, the need to create a record of my experiences continued to grow in me and would not let me rest. I felt that I had to write something about my experiences that could be used by others. However, technology has never been my strong point, and I was unable to use a computer to get my thoughts down on paper. Even after I had obtained a mini-cassette recorder, with the idea that I could at least create an "oral history" on tape, my lack of comfort with anything mechanical rendered this method unsatisfactory. Finally, as a last resort, whenever I had a few free moments, I started writing "chapters" of a potential memoir in longhand on legal pads. After several years, I had accumulated a handwritten version of this book, but it was not in any form that would be understandable by a reader.

Then, almost a decade after the appearance of the *Public Employee Press* article, Amy West Poley, director of the Joint Public Affairs Committee (JPAC), told me that Molly Sager, the director of JPAC's Institute for Senior Action (IFSA), had offered to work with me to transfer my handwritten text to a computer. Suddenly, the entire project became feasible to me, and I was off and running—starting on my first book at the tender age of 91. Molly worked enthusiastically and methodically on the first part of the book, but then her full-time job required all her time and attention. At this point, Virginia "Ginny" Shields, a fellow board member at Hunter College's Scholarship and Welfare Fund, stepped in and has been working with me ever since—always available, always full of warmth and good cheer, and, most important of all, always zealous, competent and precise in whatever she undertook. My heartfelt thanks go to Molly, Ginny and the others who have helped along the way.

It was then that good fortune shone its light in the form of an old colleague whose path had crossed mine at several junctures of my activist journey. Henry Foner had been the Educational and Welfare Director of a sector of the fur union while I was superintending that union's pioneering dental clinic, which means that I have known him for some 60 years. Because of the union's leading role in the American Jewish Labor Council (AJLC), he had also been aware of my somewhat bizarre experiences organizing that body's annual bazaars. And when I finally came to rest in the "vitamin business," Henry, who, by then, was president of his union, suggested an arrangement whereby his union's members would get a special price on our vitamin products, packaged with the union's own attractive logo. As icing on the cake, Henry and his late wife, Lorraine, turned up at various stages of my career as a senior activist. Henry had not only edited his union's publication, but he also was able to remember many of the events that I had forgotten since we had gone our respective ways. When he agreed to edit my manuscript and help guide it to publication, the entire project took a giant leap forward.

I have also had more than my share of Hunter College friends, writers and editors who have read the evolving book one, two and even three times during its path to publication. These include Meg Crahan, the distinguished historian and educator, who not only read the manuscript carefully but also made many valuable suggestions; sociology professors Ruth Sidel and Jan Poppendieck, the former of whom also helped proofread the final galleys; Rose Dobrof, the founder of the Brookdale Center for the Aging; Hadassah Gold, then president of the Hunter College Scholarship and Welfare Fund; Helene Goldfarb, a board member of both the Scholarship and Welfare Fund and the *Feminist Press*, and Eli Schwartz, Hunter College's assistant archivist, who acquainted me with the college's early history and the achievements of its pioneer students. For "The Vitamin Story" section, I thank Frank Murray, the author of the *History of the Vitamin Industry*, who reproduced and made available to me pages of his book in order to ensure my historical accuracy, and Charles "Chuck" Ringel, a second generation organic food and vitamin retailer, who has been both encouraging and helpful with his suggestions.

In my search for a publisher, I turned to Brian Lehrer, host of the show of the same name on radio station WNYC; Larry Bush, editor of *Jewish Currents* magazine, who guided that publication to its historic coupling with the Jewish fraternal organization, Workmen's Circle/Arbeter Ring, and who provided me with a "shot in the arm" by publishing a chapter of this book; Aaron Lansky, the groundbreaking founder of the National Yiddish Book Center and author of the delightful *Outwitting History*; Balz Frei, executive director of the Linus Pauling Institute; New York's indefatigable Congressman Jerry Nadler, a devoted ally to our booming senior population; Brad Olson, chief of staff for New York State Senator Liz Krueger; IFSA graduates Genevieve Cervara and Brigette Castelone; and Angelica Carpenter, founder and director of the Children's Library at California State University in Fresno—all of whom did everything possible to obtain a publisher for me, and one of whom—Larry Bush—actually succeeded in guiding me to the tender ministrations of the Ben Yehuda Press.

Others who provided staunch support included Donna Shalala, President Bill Clinton's ebullient Secretary of Health and Human Services and former president of Hunter College, and my young friend Ben Ortiz, who received one of the Hunter College Scholarship and Welfare Fund's Scholars' Scholarships, which pays full tuition fees for its recipients. Ben later went on to receive his doctorate in California and is now an assistant professor at Hunter. I am grateful, too, to my other young friends in Hunter's Welfare Rights Initiative who work diligently with single mothers; to my German-born friend, Margrit Pittman, who served as both reporter and editor for several courageous anti-Nazi publications and who furnished me with a considerable amount of valuable data; and finally, Rachel Bernstein, oral history professor at New York University, co-author with the late Debra Bernhardt of the remarkable *Ordinary People, Extraordinary Lives* and co-historian with Henry Foner of the website Labor Arts (www.laborarts.org).

My family has gone beyond the bounds of duty by providing me with both advice and editorial comments, cautioning me against my tendency to indulge in unmitigated optimism, furnishing much appreciated comfort during my periods of disappointment and producing and furthering a helpful balance through the combination of my son Bob's objectivity with his life companion Marilyn's more sympathetic subjectivity. My brother, Donald, himself a writer with some experience, has also injected a dose of realism in my reactions. And my niece, Carol Finkel, has expended considerable care and diligence in compiling a three-volume album that loyally substantiates much of what I remember.

My heartfelt gratitude goes to my trade union friends who have signaled their support by pledging to distribute copies of this work to their members: Linda Schleicher, communications director of Social Service Employees Local 371; Stuart Leibowitz, president of District Council 37's large and active retirees' organization; Nancy True, director of senior activities at Teamsters' Local 237, and many others with whom I have worked through the years.

And finally, my special thanks to that remarkably diverse group of more than 500 IFSA graduates who inspire me to continue my work for a better life for the working and middle classes of this nation and the world.

Part I: Family Beginnings

Chapter 1
Sophie's Story

MAMA NEVER HAD TIME TO TALK ABOUT HER PAST when I questioned her. She insisted she had too many pressing tasks to do in the present and too many plans to make for the future. She was not too busy, however, to tell me proudly that while in Russia, she had received a scholarship to study French and Russian. She also found time to speak glowingly about the strong bond that existed between her and her four sisters, in spite of the fact that they then lived far from each other.

Being by nature a curious child, I constantly nudged her for details about her life, and my persistence paid off. Bit by bit, she filled in some of the gaps in her story. By listening to her conversations and by helping her in her busy round of activities, I was able to piece together the details of the story of her admirable life.

She was born Sophie Levine, daughter of Peter and Anne, on January 25, 1888, in Minsk, Belarus (also known as White Russia), the youngest of five daughters. Her father operated a small saloon that catered to working class gentiles. At that time and place, the law forbade Jews from holding regular jobs. They were pretty confined to being small shopkeepers, peddlers, traders and the like.

Soon after Sophie was born, her father died from an illness the family was never able to identify, and her mother had to take over the running of the saloon in order to support her growing family. My mother's twin sister, Pearl, was sent to be raised by their maternal grandmother. One by one, the five sisters, who shared an attractiveness of both looks and spirit—the oldest, Minnie, had even won a beauty contest—were able to meet and win the hearts of young Jewish men. All five married early, even though they lacked dowries. With the exception of Mary, the third oldest of the group, they all migrated to the "Golden Land," which was what my parents and their contemporaries called America. They came not only to seek their fortunes, but also to escape the pogroms and other forms of persecution Jews faced in the old country. All five raised families that included an impressive number of professionals. All of them, except Mary, lived into their 90s, and one, Pearl, lived to 100. Mary, who had remained in Minsk, was killed by the Nazis during World War II, along with most of her family of six and their children.

Pearl and Anna wound up in Chicago, Minnie in Los Angeles and my mother, Sophie—the last to leave Minsk—in New York. Her cousin, Alexander Epstein, better known as Sander, had journeyed to New York in steerage and was among the thousands of Jewish and Italian immigrants who found employment in the then burgeoning garment industry. Within two years, by skimping on meals and saving his pennies, dimes and dollars, he was able to purchase a *schiffs carte* for steerage accommodations for Sophie. He had been writing to her at least once a week and was waiting impatiently for her.

After a stormy trip, during which she said she was nauseated much of the time, she arrived at Ellis Island, where she was closely questioned, examined physically and finally released to take her place in her new country. It was July 4, 1905, she was all of 16, and she later told me that, in her naiveté, she imagined that the firecrackers and general festivities were intended as a welcome for her and her fellow newcomers.

Soon after her arrival, she and Sander were married. Like him, she quickly found a job in the garment industry, where she joined Shirtwaistmakers' Local 25, a women's local that was later involved in the historic 1909 strike. Two years later, its members were victims of the terrible Triangle Shirt fire. Fortunately, however, Sophie was no longer working by then. She had become pregnant five years earlier with her first baby—a boy, Irving, who was born in October, 1906, three months before her 18th birthday.

The Lower East Side of Manhattan—cramped, stench-filled and overpopulated—had provided a home for Jewish immigrants since the early 1880s. By 1910, almost two million Jews had fled Czar Nicholas's tyrannical regime in Russia and oppressive regimes in other parts of Europe, and had formed the largest diaspora since the Spanish Inquisition. By the time my mother arrived in this country, many Jewish families had begun to move to Brooklyn and the Bronx. In the spring of 1913, Sophie and Sander made the trek to the southeast Bronx. By then, the family had grown to four and one-half; Irving, born in 1906, Ethel in 1908, and me, still inside my mother's womb. Between Ethel and me, my mother had lost a set of twins as a result of a miscarriage.

When our family arrived at 639 East 138th Street, the building was part of a vibrant, bustling, multicultural working class area, consisting mostly of first-generation immigrants: Jews from Eastern Europe; Italians, largely from Sicily; and some second- and third-generation German Jews, as well as some descendants of the Irish immigrants who came during the 1840s to escape the potato famine.

We lived in a recently built four-story walk-up—the middle building in a row of five similar structures, all put up by a developer to shelter part of the huge influx of immigrants who had left the overcrowded, noisy and unstable Lower East Side. The place we called home had indoor plumbing, with a private toilet and bath, hot and cold water, electricity and steam heat! Our cheerful, sun-filled, five-room apartment, which my parents had obtained with a month's free rent, was on the second floor front, facing 138th Street. Mama was really thrilled by the fact that we were finally living as a family group, even though there were times when we had to take in a boarder or two for short periods to supplement the family income. Nevertheless, it was still *ours*!

Our neighbors were pleasant and congenial and stayed put in their apartments for years. They often became friends. Lincoln Hospital was nearby where Mama would have her first child away from home (I was born there on June 18, 1913).

The schools were good, and there was even an excellent high school within walking distance. The storekeepers knew us all by name; there were local organizations within convenient reach and a park nearby where we could play. Our family lived there for 16 years, until I graduated from high school.

My mother was determined to learn to read and write English and to become a citizen, so she attended night school. She also wanted to be able to converse with all her neighbors—Jewish, Italian or Irish. She was not only an apt pupil, but she also found time to participate in the struggle for women's suffrage. When that cause was won, she was ready. She registered to vote and never neglected to do so, as she considered it both her right and her duty.

I was almost three when Mama gave birth to a bright, bubbly, blond, noisy baby boy named Harold. Before he started walking at fourteen months, he could be found crawling all over the apartment. With his birth, Mama had to cut back on her activities –after all, she had two small children to take care of. Aside from constantly bombarding her with questions, I gave her very little trouble. But even though Harold never seemed to cry, he constantly left his small toys and the pot covers he banged on all over the place, which made the apartment a minefield. Since he also liked to try to stand and climb up the tallest pieces of furniture, Mama had to watch him constantly.

One evening, when Harold was 18 months old, he suddenly developed a very high fever. Mama was frantic. She called our doctor, Joseph Edelstein, who lived across the street down the block. Harold was too sick to be taken to the doctor's office, and when Dr. Edelstein heard her describe his other symptoms, he immediately came over. He had Harold moved to the hospital at once, but, (alas!) they misdiagnosed his condition, and he died the next morning of meningitis.

Mama was inconsolable. She, so strong and so able to deal with crises, now cried constantly. For months, she stayed at home. Her friends were unable to get her to leave the apartment to attend meetings, lectures or social events. Whenever I saw her weeping, I would either put my arms around her or lay my head in her lap. I would often make matters worse by asking her when Harold was coming home. Nevertheless, my gestures of need and affection seemed to calm her, and she would pat my head and hold me tightly. She vowed that she would never have another child, and to make sure that didn't happen, for some time she refused to sleep in the same bed with Papa.

It was clear that even though Mama loved her children dearly, they came along too quickly. If she had been able to choose the time of her children's birth, she would have been able to give us more attention and still do her beloved community work. I never learned whether she knew that during that very period —in 1916—a courageous woman named Margaret Sanger had opened a birth control clinic in Brooklyn, for which she was immediately sent to jail. (Ironically, some 20 years later, I visited the main Margaret Sanger clinic in an East 16th Street brownstone to obtain my own contraceptives).

Mama was finally lured back to activity when she learned that the organization to which she belonged was launching a special campaign to fight against steeply rising food prices. In an effort to sublimate the pain of her loss, she fought harder than ever. She had already joined the Socialist Consumers League (SCL), a group of courageous housewives and mothers. This was hardly surprising, since many immigrants had been exposed to socialist writings. Her organization policed the local stores to guarantee that prices were competitive, encouraged the organizing of tenants and led rent strikes. In this way, they sought to make sure that they would be able to stretch their meager incomes to be able to pay the rent and buy food for their families. My mother's activity in these campaigns won her a gold pin, with her name engraved on it, from her organization.

World War I, which was taking place at this time, is memorable to me because of the food rationing that was in effect. Mama, however, was able to make tasty brown honey cakes without using sugar. We saved rubber bands, rolled them into balls for play in the streets and gave them to the older children. We also rolled tin foil into balls and contributed them to the war effort.

It was shortly after the war that Mama's moment of heroic activity took place. Prices had risen sharply, and since there was no rent control, landlords were able to raise rents excessively. Real estate had become a major form of investment, and people who had been able to save were buying income-producing apartment houses. One such person, an independent house painter, who had accumulated money by paying low wages to his unorganized workers, bought the house in which we lived. With an eye toward making a "killing," he immediately raised rents to levels that were higher than most of the tenants could afford to pay.

After negotiations proved futile, my mother organized a rent strike. Half the tenants refused to pay their rent, depositing it instead in an escrow account. As a result, 10 families, including ours, were evicted by a city marshal and all of our belongings put out on the street. Fortunately, it was a warm day in July. There was a feeling of general euphoria among the tenants because of the broad support the strike was receiving from the neighborhood. At least a hundred people were standing in the street, booing the marshal and applauding the evicted families. As a result, what started out as a disaster turned, instead, into the equivalent of a street fair. The evictees arranged their furniture on the street in front of the five houses that were part of the original development. Refreshments were provided by the evicted tenants from their hastily emptied iceboxes and by sympathetic neighbors and friends.

While my mother and a *pro bono* lawyer were busy in court, my older sister, 12 or 13 by then, played jazz on a piano. Everyone in the street danced, sang and talked excitedly about what was going on. I moved from group to group, explaining my mother's absence and experiencing a new sense of importance. That night, while the case was still being argued, the evictees' families slept in other people's homes, or on the sidewalk, either on chairs or on hastily assembled beds.

The next day, we learned that we had won the court case. The judge ruled that the rent increases were exorbitant and awarded a modest increase to the landlord. We returned to our apartments in triumph. I was bursting with pride over my mother's role, and I was not averse to sharing the congratulations heaped upon her by all the neighbors.

PRACTICALLY EVERY SMALL COMMUNITY has its own gossip mechanism—busy, buzzing, middle-aged (everyone else is middle-aged when you are less than 10 years old) ladies circulating the undercover news around—and our housing complex was no exception. We had few telephones available and certainly no e-mails, but Lily, Mary, Rachel and Evelyn—Mary tall and thin, and the other three short and round—carried out their tasks of gathering and dispensing information conscientiously and effectively. Cuckolded husbands, wandering wives, alcoholics—all were reported on regularly—but our East 138th Street complex provided a very special subject for their activities: a 29-year-old spinster named Esther (a characteristic odd enough by itself), who was both the executive secretary and mistress of a leading realtor. Every Thursday evening at 11 o'clock, she would arrive alone at her front door in the second building of our complex in a Rolls-Royce, bid the driver "good night" and hurry upstairs to her apartment. Sometimes, after a business trip, she would come home during the day—always in the Rolls-Royce. Needless to say, her comings and goings were the subject of endless conjecture.

Esther, petite with lovely skin and eloquent eyes, was not particularly pretty, but she exuded elegance. She wore delicate, hand-made silk blouses and simple, soft wool, black, brown or blue custom-made suits, all fashioned by her employer's tailor. She was rumored to own two French designer dresses for formal occasions. She lived with her brother, Max, and her parents; her father a low-level official in a neighborhood synagogue, and her hard-working mother, who kept her apartment spotlessly clean, washing the kitchen linoleum every day, on her hands and knees, and covering it with the previous day's newspaper. She never failed to greet me with a freshly baked cookie, often still warm from the oven.

The gossip crew was determined to learn more about their mysterious neighbor. They tried to enlist Mama in their fact-finding enterprise, especially after they saw her leaving the family's apartment on more than one occasion. But Mama was adamant in her refusal to cooperate, insisting that, as the housing representative, she made it a practice to visit all the tenants. She expressed her contempt for the gossipers, insisting that all they did was interfere with the constructive work that had to be done and that they could make better use of their time on a picket line. (Mama always felt that picketing was a means for solving every conceivable problem).

Mama did, however, find a very concrete use for Esther's real estate expertise. One day, unable to find the answer to a current rental situation from her usual sources, she called Esther on the phone, and was invited to come to see her. Esther graciously shared her information with Mama, and thereafter, Mama and I would visit her whenever the need arose to consult her on tenant problems. I was sworn to secrecy about these visits, since Mama was unyielding in her determination not to provide any grist for the gossipers' mill. In fact, this is the first time I have ever mentioned it.

And then, one day, just as quietly as they had come into the complex, Esther's family moved out—hopefully to a location where they would be immune to gossip.

Chapter 2
Sander's Story

IN A PICTURE THAT STILL HANGS ON MY BEDROOM WALL, I can see a slender, handsome, olive-skinned man, of medium height and with a shock of black hair, a full, black mustache and bright, friendly dark brown eyes. He is not smiling because, even though he is only in his mid-20s, his habit of chain-smoking homemade cigarettes made of thin paper rolled around cheap tobacco has already discolored his teeth.

Little is known of Papa's background and early life. He was an extremely private person, and, even when prodded, was reluctant to talk about himself. Nevertheless, there emerged the outlines of a story that was similar to those of countless other Eastern European Jews. We knew that Mama and he were first cousins, his father being Mama's mother's brother. Like her, he was born in Minsk. At the age of 15, he was conscripted into the army. After two years, he deserted; he was caught and imprisoned along with many revolutionaries, most of whom were anarchists. He was profoundly affected by their idealism and energy. Like so many other hopeful, disenchanted Jews in Russia at the time, he longed to come to America for a better and more fulfilling life. In 1903, at the age of 23, he left Russia for America, after assuring Mama, then almost 15, that he loved her and would send for her as soon as possible.

At Ellis Island, his given name was changed. Although he was named Alexander, all his friends and relatives called him "Sander." However, the clerk who interviewed him upon his arrival converted "Sander" to "Sam," and so it remained for the rest of his life, even in legal documents. Mama, however, always addressed him as "Sander."

On the ocean journey to the United States, Sander met two young men his own age. One of them, Ben, was planning to stay with a cousin who lived on Eldridge Street in the Lower East Side and who, Ben was told, would be able to find him a job in the garment industry. Sander and the other young man, named Boris, decided to tag along with Ben, and a warm friendship developed among the three young men. They lived together for two years, and even though their lives later took different paths, they maintained contact with one another for many years.

Papa joined the thousands of other semi-skilled garment workers whom employers were eagerly seeking in what was becoming the fastest growing industry in New York City. They had to work long hours—sometimes as many as 80 a week —at low piecework rates and in a squalid and physically dangerous environment. As a result, these workers, already both idealistic and politically aware, were ripe for organization. When the cloakmakers' union was established in 1900 with the aim of organizing a union of all crafts within the ladies' garment industry, it was granted a charter by the American Federation of Labor (AFL) and called the International Ladies' Garment Workers' Union, or ILGWU. My father was among its earliest members and he worked hard to convince others to join. He later told me that he often used the old refrain, "You have nothing to lose but your chains."

Papa was active in the huge 1910 strike of 60,000 garment workers that won a 50-hour week and an end to what was called "inside shop subcontracting." This was a particularly infuriating workers' grievance. Under it, a supervisor, or some other person, would "handle" the work assignments of a group of workers— which meant that he would enjoy the equivalent of a "kickback" of a portion of those workers' pay.

From early on, Papa was an active participant in the "left-wing" opposition in his local, which was one of the largest in the union. Both on and off season, he was constantly active and was always attending one meeting or another to help plan strategy. Because he was an anarchist, he refused to accept any paid job in the local, claiming that it would make him vulnerable to the corruption that was rife at the time. He even refused to take such unpaid jobs as shop chairman or delegate.

A major strike in 1926 for shorter hours and better pay ended disastrously for the union. Papa had been most outspoken in his opposition to the employers and after the strike was over, his continuing participation in the opposition did not sit well with the leaders of the union. As a result, he was "blacklisted" and was not able to obtain a regular job. It became harder and harder for Mama to manage. During the eight years after I graduated from college in 1933, we moved six times, first further north, then further east, then back again—each time seeking lower rents and the "concessions" of several months' free rent. Between home relief, odd jobs, and taking in boarders, we managed to survive.

Just prior to this period, our family experienced the joy of the marriage of my older sister, Ethel, to a federal customs house inspector named Max Lewis. Since they both wanted a big wedding and we could not afford a hall with a caterer, Mama coaxed our janitor into letting us use the empty apartment next door. We decorated the walls and fixtures with brightly colored crepe paper. A neighbor baked a large chocolate layer cake. Mama, too, baked, and between our friends and Ethel's, we had enough food and drink to make it a memorable occasion. My brother Irving and two of his friends provided music for dancing. Ethel looked just lovely in an orange and green chiffon print dress. It was well past midnight when we finally bade the guests good night.

PAPA WAS A MAN OF DEEP EMOTIONS. He adored his wife and loved his family. While I was searching for details about our early family life, my younger brother, Donald, told me that when he was about five years old, Papa would bring home some trinkets for him, which he gave him after teasing him by hiding them and making him find them. Papa also told him funny jokes and carried him around on his shoulders. However, there were evenings when he would endlessly pace the floor in our hallway, chain smoking and just worrying...worrying...worrying.

During the "off-season," Papa, who liked to design dresses in addition to his regular work as an operator, would sometimes find some pieces of fine material and make a simple dress for

Mama or a fancy one for Ethel. As a high school graduation gift, he gave me a lovely black silk dress with wine-colored satin cuffs and collar.

One feature of our family life that distinguished us and a surprisingly large number of other immigrant families from other Jewish families was the fact that we did not follow the usual practice of favoring the male members over the girls. My parents both encouraged all four children to go to college and to study and study some more. Papa had been unable to attend school, but he had learned to read and write both Yiddish and Russian. As I mentioned, Mama had received a scholarship to study French and Russian. Whenever they wanted to discuss something they didn't want us to comprehend, they spoke in Russian. While we could understand most of their Yiddish, their Russian went way over our heads. However, we were acute enough to realize that when they spoke in Russian, it was a sign of some kind of trouble.

Both of my parents were deeply disappointed when neither Ethel nor Irving graduated from high school. However, both Donald and I did and went on to graduate from college— Donald with the help of the G.I. Bill of Rights and I through the combination of free tuition, a scholarship and a Saturday job.

Even when the garment industry, through the infusion provided by Franklin D. Roosevelt's New Deal and its National Recovery Administration, experienced a period of rapid growth, there was no decent job available for Papa, who was still feeling the effects of the blacklist. He had to turn to the New Deal's Works Project Administration (WPA) for work—and then only as a manual laborer. He had to accept a job for which he was simply not physically prepared. In January, 1940, at the age of 59, he succumbed to pneumonia. When he was taken to Montefiore Hospital, they learned that he had lung cancer, which metastasized rapidly and spread to his brain. After an unsuccessful operation to remove the tumor, he died—a man who had been unable, despite his best efforts, to help achieve a better world for mankind. Instead, as a result of his radical activity, he had only made life more difficult for his family. He was thoroughly disillusioned by the corruption he observed among the leaders of the union that he loved. Nevertheless, he maintained a deep sense of pride at having remained true to his principles. It was a pride that all of us shared. And I, particularly, both appreciated and learned much from his energy, his humor, his compassion and his love of beautiful things.

Part II
Growing Up in the Southeast Bronx

Chapter 3
The Sights, Sounds and Smells—and the Food

MANY OF OUR DAYS BEGAN with the ritual of walking five blocks to Southern Boulevard and East 141st Street to purchase "day-old" bread at Ward's bakery. Ward's was a nationally known company that made packaged bread. While we patiently queued up for the 10-cent loaves, our nostrils were soothed by the warm scent of baking bread.

Sunday was by far the best day of the week. Then, we would stand on a much smaller line of neighborhood patrons who were waiting to buy fresh, just-baked rolls, either plain or poppy-seeded, for two cents each at the German bakery that stood just across the street from our apartment building. You could always tell the garment season from the type of rolls we purchased and ate. During the busy season, when Papa was working, we would eat sweet rolls with the chicory-mixed coffee that was always boiling on our stove. These included such delicacies as rich cinnamon buns, multiflavored jelly rolls and the delicious coffee-cake squares that had, at the very last moment, been sprinkled with confectioner's sugar. Here, the smells were far more tantalizing and seductive than in the commercial bakery. I had trained myself to walk past the French pastry showcase, although I must confess that I would sometimes steal a glance at these "forbidden fruits." These were the highest-priced items, far beyond our pocketbooks. But we were satisfied with what we were able to buy and we would rush home to devour our Sunday treats.

During the garment industry's season, when money was available, we would descend the hill on 138th Street to St. Ann's Avenue. There, the so-called "appetizing" store (and its contents were indeed appetizing) sold such delicacies as smoked salmon, familiarly known as lox, smoked whitefish, sable, sturgeon, marinated and matjes herring, and mouth-watering pickles that floated in brine and dill. My sister Ethel and I would buy a quarter-pound of lox for 39 cents, or sometimes a small, fat whitefish. As the youngest (at least until my brother, Donald, was born), I was permitted to lick the tidbits remaining on the skin after the fish was sliced.

When Papa worked overtime, there were other special treats, like a Sunday mid-day dinner of breaded veal cutlets with home-fried potatoes and cooked peas. Then our entire family, Papa, Mama, Ethel, Irving and I—dressed in our Sunday best—would walk to 149th Street and Third Avenue, known as "The Hub," the home of the Royal Theater, to see a live vaudeville show. We would spend the afternoon laughing at the comedians and gaping with wonderment at the magicians, acrobats and aerial artists.

Mama was only a mediocre cook. She admitted that she didn't enjoy doing it, but she dutifully prepared dinner for us every day before she went off, either to a meeting or to night school. Whenever possible, she ate with us, and on those occasions, we dined as a family in the kitchen on a table I had proudly set. Her *chef d'oeuvre* was old-fashioned pot roast—a boneless chuck steak, cooked and then simmered with carrots, tomatoes and chunky baby potatoes. Oddly enough, it always tasted better, reheated, the next day.

On Mondays, rare hamburger, enhanced by crushed bread, grated carrots and tomato sauce, was a regular weekly routine (I actually liked it raw, so Mama always saved a small patty for me). On Tuesdays, there was homemade soup and beef liver with sautéed onions. On Wednesdays, we had pot roast. Thursday was "leftover day," supplemented by potatoes and perhaps some homemade pea soup. On Friday night, in keeping with Jewish custom, we had boiled chicken in hot chicken soup, to which were added two cents' worth of soup greens, a fresh carrot and carefully scrubbed chicken feet for flavoring. Because fish was inexpensive, we often started our meals with boiled carp or whitefish, flavored with onions and carrots, or with fried flounder. And for a marvelous Saturday lunch, there was either cold chicken or cold fish.

When I was quite young, Mama would take me with her on Friday mornings to the chicken market on 137th Street and Brook Avenue. There, housewives would choose a live chicken to be slaughtered by the *shochet*, the kosher meat killer, and then dressed by a plucker. Or else, they would select from an assortment of already dressed chickens hanging from a beam on hooks. The birds were classified for roasting, frying or boiling to make soup.

The scene was always noisy and frenetic—a mixture of cackling, frightened hens and women haggling loudly. Chickens ran frantically back and forth over the straw-strewn floor, while bloody-aproned pluckers, who were paid by the piece, deftly pulled the large feathers, then the fine pinfeathers from the freshly killed fowl. Other workers weighed, eviscerated and then cut up the bird, under the purchaser's watchful eye, making sure that nothing she wanted was removed. The *shochet* waited patiently between jobs, while what seemed to me to be hundreds of busy women carefully scrutinized the hanging birds, feeling, poking and pinching them for unhatched eggs or testing them for plumpness, the size of their breasts, or the flatness of their thighs—all the while exchanging, in high-pitched tones, comments with their neighbors and with the sharp-tongued salespersons. I must confess that I was as terrified as the chickens, and I held on tight to Mama's hand. Later, I would stand at a safe distance in the far corner, watching the scene, wide-eyed and curious.

On Fridays, too, we would wend our way through the many pushcarts, owned or rented mostly by Jewish and a few Italian peddlers, which lined the sidewalks the entire length of the block outside the chicken market. There, we bought soup greens, bags of apples and potatoes, and, in season, beets and cabbage for the delicious soups that Mama remembered from her Russian home. Sometimes bananas and oranges were on sale. It was not until I was of school age that Mama learned about salad greens, cucumbers and tomatoes. She had her favorite vendors whom she patronized regularly. They, in turn, were captivated by her warm smile and inherent geniality and gave her special treatment—a taste of something new or a special bargain. On other occasions, especially during the summer, a horse-drawn fruit and vegetable wagon would come by our street. The driver would proclaim his wares, loudly and unintelligibly. We may not have known what he was shouting, but we certainly were able to see what he had. In no time, a group of women would congregate at the curb, all talking at once. Sometimes, it was just one item—watermelon, perhaps—sold by the slice, quarter, half or whole. More often, the wagon would be loaded with multicolored fresh fruits and vegetables, straight from the farm.

Even though we disagreed over just about everything else, my siblings and I never fought over who got what part of the chicken. Mama always chose a bird with ample thighs. I preferred the dark meat, so I got a leg. Both Ethel and Irving liked the white meat, so each got a wing and part of the breast. Papa took the other leg, while Mama gathered the odds and ends, sucked on the chicken feet, and ate that portion of the chicken liver that she had not chopped up and served as an appetizer, along with a hard-boiled egg, onion and chicken fat. Unhatched eggs were a rare delicacy, to be cooked in the soup. If there was more than one, I, as the youngest, was the lucky recipient—one of the bonuses that came with the territory.

WHEN PAPA WAS NOT WORKING, we would frequently have organ meats for our main course. These beef parts, now a luxury in the finest continental restaurants where they are sold as sweetbreads, tripe and kidneys, were often discarded by the butcher and offered to a preferred customer to be given to her cat. On many an evening, this "cat food" served as our nourishment, although we eased our consciences by giving Patty, our cat, some of the scraps.

My favorite dish was potato pancakes, familiarly known as *latkes*, a Yiddish word, which seems to aptly describe the thin, crusty fried batter that Mama dropped into very hot oil and turned over very quickly with a flat spatula. In what seemed less than a minute, she would take them out of the pan and drop them on absorbent paper towels to drain the excess fat. We often grabbed them before they even reached our plates, burning our fingers in our eagerness. I found them extraordinarily tasty, and I willingly helped Mama by peeling the potatoes. I peeled and she grated and then mixed in an egg; and I can still savor the indescribably satisfying crunch of a crisp biteful. We sometimes added homemade applesauce, made from damaged apples that had been carefully cut and peeled.

When I was five or six years old, I would look forward with great anticipation to the evenings when Papa came home directly from work. Often, he stayed downtown for a union meeting or to help plan strategy with his fellow shop workers. When he came home early, I picked up the aluminum beer can and accompanied him to the German saloon at 140th Street and Cypress Avenue, two blocks from our home. It was an old-fashioned saloon with all the features—a mahogany bar, leaded glass, colored windows and swinging doors.

We would be greeted by the rich, pungent odors of limburger, cheddar and Gruyère cheeses that were offered free to the patrons. Beer was constantly flowing from the many spigots lining the inside of the bar. On the other side, German, Irish, Italian and Jewish workers sat and quaffed their beer, enjoying the warm camaraderie of kindred souls before returning home to their families. The air was filled with the hum of clamorous, yet friendly conversation. I learned that for many of these men, this gathering was a daily ritual.

While Papa was occupied having the bartender fill his can with the foaming beer, I would reach up over the bar and grasp a handful of the flavorful cheeses. Occasionally, we would bring some home for Mama and the other family members.

I would always know when Papa was back at work after the "dry" season. He would bring home a new Caruso record and play it immediately on our portable phonograph, while he sang along with the famous tenor whose beautiful voice resonated through the room with arias from *Pagliacci, Aida, Rigoletto, The*

Jewess, and other operatic favorites. He would also bring home framed reproductions of then popular well-known paintings, such as *The Gleaners* by Jean-François Millet, *September Morn*, and an anonymous still-life portraying a large slice of watermelon, two oranges and some ripe peaches. This last was, appropriately enough, hung on the wall in the kitchen, above the table.

Although Mama loved opera and would sometimes even join in the singing, she would also grumble, *sotto voce*, and sometimes even out loud. She was the more practical of the two. After all, she was the one who had to face the impatient grocer and butcher, demanding that their bills get paid. Somehow, mysteriously, these tradesmen were the first to know when the work season had begun. Because it was she who bore the brunt of these awkward encounters, Mama sometimes complained about Papa spending his hard-earned money on what she called "unnecessities." However, he felt that life was so stressful that it was necessary at times to relieve its strains with some audible or visible expression of beauty. On the other hand, he heartily approved of Mama's practice of putting aside small amounts of money for the causes she held dear.

Another of Papa's personal indulgences was card-playing. He enjoyed spending Thursday evenings playing pinochle with his union cronies. Included in that group was a recently-appeared first cousin, Harry Epstein, the son of his father's brother and a member of the Furriers' Union who had moved to the Bronx. No matter how difficult the times or how pressing the problems, Thursday evenings were sacrosanct. Mama, on the other hand, hated the card games. It was not the time away from home that troubled her, but rather the money that could be better used for food or in support of a worthy cause. Oddly enough, this seemingly minor issue became the source of some of their bitterest discussions. I was always disturbed by the sharpness of their tones and the harshness of their words. The issue was resolved, however, when Papa became too tired, and later, too ill to go anywhere in the evenings. But it left its mark on me: I never learned to play cards and I have never gambled.

Before escaping from the Russian army, Papa had been a captain's orderly. He had captivated that officer by playing the mandolin and singing mournful Russian songs: *Dark Eyes, The Birch Tree,* and *The Volga Boatman* among them. On Sunday mornings, he would play the mandolin at home and sing Russian songs, revolutionary chants and Jewish folk melodies in his rich baritone. Mama and I would add our voices to the chorus, and these were among the times I relished most.

DURING THE WINTER, WHEN MAMA WAS AT HOME, I hurried home from school for a hot lunch. Mama would prepare a bowl of steaming Campbell's tomato soup, its thickness diluted by fresh milk, or a platter of buttered noodles with pot cheese. Often, there was one of the special cereals I enjoyed most: gritty yellow corn meal thickly covered with pot cheese. We used huge quantities of this latter item because it was the least expensive of the cheeses we liked. For summer lunches, Mama would plunk pot cheese into thick, rich sour cream. Sour cream, too, was a favorite, serving, as it did, as a refreshing base for berries, bananas or tomatoes and cucumbers. On rainy days, I took along sandwiches of kummel-sprinkled Jewish rye bread, filled with Swiss, Muenster or farmer cheese, or a hard-boiled egg.

Mama's favorite grocery was Mr. Plotkin's, one of three stores at the corner of Cypress Avenue and 138th Street. The owner kept a wide variety of products, the store was conveniently located and Mr. Plotkin offered credit accounts for those families, including ours, that had to go through lean seasons. This served the same purpose as credit cards do today and Mr. Plotkin, a compassionate man, charged no interest. Mama bought all her dairy products and staples there. Mr. Plotkin kept his records on numerous strips of white paper, one for each family. After adding up the items with a pencil stub on the outside of the brown paper bag in which the groceries were packed, he put the total on the appropriate strip and then placed it back in the drawer under the cash register. He would count and recount the items to make sure that nothing was omitted or duplicated. The brown bag served as the verification of the transaction. Even when I was quite young, I was able to do the marketing. Mama would prepare a list that I showed to the grocer. Although the store was close to our home, with no streets to cross, I sometimes had to return a second time if the load was too heavy.

Mrs. Dart, an ailing neighbor, had all her major groceries delivered once a week. Since her husband had steady employment, she always paid cash and thereby earned this special service. If she either forgot or ran out of an item, she would send me to buy it for her. In this way, I earned my pennies for the candy I bought at the candy store right next door to the grocer—a wonderful, sweet world of hundreds of sugary confections and honeyed smells. A more unreliable source of my tips was Mrs. Orzeck, across the hall, a young Polish woman with a small baby, who sometimes forgot necessary items while she was shopping.

Sometimes, when I was feeling lucky, I would put a penny into the gumball machine near the door of the store. When you turned the handles, the brightly colored balls rolled around and around. If an orange ball bounced out, you would win five cents' worth of candy. The balls, themselves, were not very tasty, but the attraction was the chance to win a prize. I never did. Whenever I turned the lever, I would get red, yellow, green and purple balls—but never an orange one. I finally decided that the only way I would get the five-cent Hershey almond bar, or a strawberry ice cream cone, was by saving my pennies. It was a lesson I never forgot.

EVEN THOUGH WE WERE SECULAR, we were, like many of our neighbors, proudly Jewish. We followed European Jewish eating patterns, but, unlike our more observant neighbors, we had only one set of dishes. However, we never mixed dairy and meat foods. Mama's rational explanation for this was that they didn't taste good together. "Imagine," she would say, making a face, "having milk with meat! " (Until very recently, I had operated on the same principle, but I learned within a very short time that I actually liked the combination).

Despite Papa's ill-concealed disdain, Mama followed other traditions. She sometimes took me all the way downtown by subway to the home of her uncle, Haim Levine, on East 14th Street for Passover services. Haim was a older, kindly Jewish gentleman who had a long, partially gray beard and was firmly grounded in the classical Jewish literature. He always wore a *yarmulke*.

Whatever their minor disagreements, however, my parents were firm in their belief that *all* people are created equal and they never showed any evidence of partiality for or against any group. They vigorously opposed such tendencies whenever they manifested themselves.

Chapter 4
More Food, Friends and Neighbors

EVEN THOUGH ETHEL WAS JUST FIVE YEARS OLDER THAN I, and Irving seven, we might as well have been generations apart, so little did we have in common with respect to interests, outlook and values. Ethel was tall—five feet, six inches—svelte and blonde, with gray-green eyes and long, well-shaped legs. She was flamboyant and always in good spirits. By her sheer energy and exuberance, she would dominate any group she was in. She loved dramatic clothes, bold makeup, jazz, movies, cars, boys, dancing and fun. She was bright, but she chose Morris High School, with its lower educational standards, because it was co-educational.

During a summer vacation at age 16, she obtained a job in Bloomingdale's linen department and never went back to high school. And when Mama pleaded with her to finish high school, she was quick to respond: "You know how hard it is to get work. You also know that Papa doesn't make enough during the season to last out the year. You need some help, and I need extra money for the clothes that Papa doesn't make for me. At school, they've already taught me to read, write and speak English, but they didn't teach me how to get a good paying job. That I'll have to do for myself. Besides, I like selling—it puts me in contact with people and gives me an opportunity to influence them. Dorothy loves school. Let her go on. I don't want to." And she agreed to pay 10 dollars a month to help cover expenses.

Irving, somewhat taller than Ethel, had light brown, curly hair, gray-blue eyes and a shy smile. While he was much more studious than Ethel and had a much better school record, they enjoyed each other's company, shared each other's friends and frequently went out together socially. Of the two, Ethel was the dominant one. Irving had won a bronze medal in an essay contest sponsored by the *Bronx Home News* (which I have just recently discovered) and was admitted to Stuyvesant High School, which, even then, was considered a major accomplishment and where he was an honor student. Nevertheless, he shared Ethel's attitude toward the value of education. He felt that he needed to improve his jazz playing on the piano in order to get better "gigs," and, despite Mama and Papa's pleading, he left his prestigious high school just before graduation in order to pursue a career as a jazz pianist in a newly-formed band.

My sister and brother's feeling about the importance of education was hardly unusual. All children growing up in our surroundings during that period wanted to do something to help sustain their families, whether it was running errands, shining shoes or hawking newspapers—anything to prepare them to obtain their working papers. when they reached the magic age of sixteen, at which point their efforts to secure regular employment became even more intense.

In spite of her negative feelings about school, Ethel was always a leader among her friends. Even when they played the game of pupils and teacher, she was the teacher. And when, later in life, her daughter went to elementary school, Ethel headed the Parent-Teachers' Association and was responsible for a number of improvements, both in school and in the community, which she reported to us with great pride.

Another characteristic shared by Ethel and Irving was their unwillingness to be involved in any form of politics, for, while they respected Mama for her activities, they also resented her for the time it took her away from the family. Irving's aversion to politics did not carry over into his musical career, for he joined and was a loyal member of Local 802 of the Musicians' Union.

Unlike me, Ethel's and Irving's interests lay in making as much money as they could, which was little enough in those days. If they could achieve this at jobs that they enjoyed doing, so much the better. Ethel was a typical "flapper" of the period —the term applied to young women of her day who loved dancing, riding in roadsters with the top down and going to parties. It was at one such party that Ethel met her future husband, Mac, who, true to form, owned a red roadster.

Ethel's life style helped introduce me to at least one kind of pleasure. Cy Peltz, the oldest son of one of our top-floor neighbors, was a perfume salesman for a Japanese importer, and he used the products of his trade as a means of winning Ethel's favor. Even today, the distinctive smell of sandalwood or the strong odor of musk bring back to me recollections of the small sample bottles of perfume tucked into the lacquered red and black containers that were bestowed upon Ethel by her sales-man-suitor.

I would stealthily sneak short sniffs or apply secret dabs of those fragrances, which were displayed on Mama's dresser, and, if the truth be known, I probably derived more satisfaction from them than Ethel. The reader must remember that this was during the 1920s, when the young and the well-heeled spent freely on their favorite fragrances: Chanel No. 5; White Shoulders, the delicate gardenia preparation; the well-advertised Arpège by Lanvin ("Promise her anything, but give her Arpège!"); Shalimar by Guerlain; and so many other scents, some of which have become, by now, casualties of the fickle fates of fashion.

Throughout my later years, I continued to use these exotic-smelling creations (my favorite was Mitsouka by Guerlain) whenever I would go out after work on Saturday evenings. I would also enjoy buying both well-known and unknown brands of toilet water for customers, friends and relatives alike, as special gifts.

Ethel's clothing needs presented a professional challenge to Papa, who responded by fashioning unusual outfits for her. I remember a striking black satin, sleeveless, straight-line dress, trimmed with three rows of white monkey fur and topped with a three-quarter length lined cape of the same material, simi-larly edged. She wore this outfit whenever she wanted to make a special impression—and that was quite often. The dress is long gone, but her daughter still keeps the cape for remembrance.

Ethel would allow me, her kid sister, to tag along when she went shopping on Sunday mornings, but never let me join in her games or other activities. "Grow up first," she told me, and grow up I did, but she was always five years older, and she never let me forget it. As a result, I developed my own friends, which was relatively easy. Many of the families in our five-building complex—Jews, both religious and assimilated, Germans, Italians and Irish—included at least one child my age. We played together, read together, studied together and sometimes ate together when a hospitable neighbor would invite me in for an after-school snack or sometimes even for an entire meal. I took pride in expanding my food vocabulary and it soon included a more extensive Jewish component, along with some entirely new ethnic dishes.

I noticed that when I was invited to dinner on Fridays in the home of East European Jewish immigrants (I knew they were Jewish, because they had the same accents as my parents), they would all set out identical main dishes: chicken soup, chicken and often chopped liver. It didn't matter if they were secular and never went to synagogue, like us, or went only on important holidays, or if they went every Saturday and lit candles every Friday evening. The menu varied only slightly. Often, the chicken was roasted or the dessert changed from cooked fruit to an array of cakes—but the basic ingredients remained the same. The fact that the chicken and fish were served cold on Saturday, since no fire could be lit to warm the food, only served to reinforce my theory.

I checked with Bella Fishman, Mama's good friend, and she told me, "It's our link to the old country. It helps us remember the good things in our past." One person I asked said it was a tradition that held the Jews together, since they were spread all over the map. Another said, "We always ate that way, and it's good to continue and to see my neighbors do the same. Why should I change?" It had become a tradition—with its roots, perhaps, in religion—but it was not necessarily remembered that way. And lo and behold! "chicken soup" has entered our general vocabulary as the dish that cures all ills.

DURING THOSE EARLY YEARS, my closest friend was Bertha Gustafero, the youngest daughter in the Italian family who lived across the hall from us. Because she was frail and sickly (she had been born prematurely, after a long period of labor, and she was always suffering from some illness or other), we spent many afternoons together, reading Andersen's and Grimm's fairy tales, Greek and Roman mythology, the multi-volumed saga of the Bobbsey Twins, and the rags-to-riches tales of Horatio Alger. Sitting together in Bertha's bedroom, which she shared with two of her many sisters, we dreamed of far-off kingdoms and happy endings in which the two of us, poor scullery maids just like Cinderella, would marry the handsome prince. We reveled in the stirring amorous exploits of Zeus, ruler of the gods, Minerva, goddess of Wisdom, and Venus, the goddess of Love.

Her mother, tall, gaunt and indefatigable, with piercing brown eyes, would cook literally pounds of endlessly long spaghetti in a three-foot-high vat, and would allow the rich, Sicilian tomato sauce to simmer all night. I savored her pasta *al dente*. She was continually working. Between stirrings and tastings, she could be seen sewing in the dark dining room, beading intricate designs on black, silk fabric stretched out on a frame. Except for Bertha, when the six daughters came home from either school or work, they would join their mother in her work in order to enable her to complete her current contracted homework. She was always ready for the next batch, which was delivered every Friday morning.

Mrs. Gustafero was determined to transform her progeny from the children of Italian immigrants into respected American professionals. Even though she had no sons, she was convinced that her intelligent, industrious daughters would be able to fill that gap. She toiled, she scrimped, she encouraged, she cajoled and she ordered—all in her forceful Italian. The two oldest, Margaret and Elizabeth, were already attending Hunter College in the evening after working during the day. Later, they both went on to receive their doctoral degrees. When last I heard, Margaret was teaching at Hunter, Elizabeth was a professor at an out-of-town university, Helen had become a social worker and Eleanor a bookkeeper. Mary, two years older than

Bertha, was a fellow student of mine in a special class in high school.

My closest "outdoor" friend was Lois Berman, a fourth generation German Jew on her mother's side. She lived with her parents and her younger brother, Harold, in a five-room, front apartment on a first floor that glowed with sunshine. Lois was a "C" student, more interested in outdoor games than in books. On clear days, she and I went outdoors to play hopscotch, stoop ball, jacks and one-two-three-O'Leary-bounce-ball, or we would skip rope. We would also join other children in games of punch ball, hide-and-seek and prisoner's base. Because of her athleticism, she was always picked before me in all the group games, but I still liked her very much. She never rubbed it in when she beat me and she was always good-natured and cheerful.

The teams of girls and boys always played separately, but when the boys' team was short a player, they would ask Lois to join them. It was in Lois's home that I first tasted such delicacies as ham, shrimp scampi and pork chops, which, like other Jewish families, my mother had never served (we couldn't afford them anyway). Lois's mother also introduced me to a number of other American dishes that she had learned to incorporate into her family's meals: chicken pot pie, large salads, sirloin steaks and baked beans.

Mrs. Berman was proud of her husband's status as an accountant in a large firm, and she drew attention to her exalted position with her polished nails and the sculpted waves of her carefully marcelled hair, done each week in a beauty parlor. Whenever I rang their bell, she invited me in and appeared genuinely pleased that I was a friend of her daughter. Perhaps she thought that being in my company would cause Lois to absorb my studious habits.

Sylvia Reitman was a classmate in many of my grammar school grades. She lived in the last house in the complex—the one nearest St. Luke's Church—and from her second-floor window, you could see all the way down the block to St. Ann's Avenue. Sylvia was both fat and bashful, but she had the face of an angel, big gray eyes, a clear complexion and berry-red, exquisitely shaped lips. She and I would usually go to the library together after school on Thursdays. Despite her girth, she was the fastest "double-dutch" jumper on the block. She was able to defeat nearly all the kids who challenged her, once her reputation had spread. Her mother, an Orthodox Jew, would offer me butter cookies, sometimes topped with crushed peanuts. Sylvia always left our games early on Friday so that she could help her mother with the Sabbath preparations.

The street was our playground. We used the sidewalk for our chalk games, for skipping rope and for our circle and song games, many of which we brought home from the school playground. For hide-and-seek, we used the cellars. Even though 138th Street was a main thoroughfare, we were able to use the center roadway for stickball, softball, prisoner's base and Red Rover. Occasionally, we would have to move aside to let a car, truck or trolley pass. Unlike most neighborhoods today, the air in ours was filled with the sounds of kids laughing, shouting, arguing and cheering and mothers yelling down from the windows. There was a constant litany of "Lillie—or Mary—or Frances, your mother wants you!" Lillie, or Mary, or Frances would have to leave the game to run an errand or "come upstairs immediately!" We may have disagreed, but we never disobeyed. I was relatively fortunate. After we moved into a back apartment, Mama would have to go to a neighbor's home in order to call me.

Sometimes, a few of us would go to St. Mary's Park on Cypress Avenue and 143rd Street to go down the sliding ponds, to fly high on the big swings, to ride the see-saws or to climb the exercise bars and jungle gyms.

Mrs. Dart, our elderly, childless, thin-as-a-board next-door neighbor, enthralled me with her brewed-for-hours tea, to which she added milk and three teaspoonfuls of sugar. You could always hear a pot of tea steaming on her stove. When I would return from an errand, she would often ask me to join her for a cup, which she served on her kitchen table in creamy

Beleek porcelain cups, adorned with delicate, green four-leaf clovers. She would offer me homemade biscuits and Irish soda bread with strawberry jam (also homemade), which she served on similarly ornamented plates.

She told me proudly that her mother had brought a complete dinner service for 12 over from Ireland when she had fled to the United States from the terrible potato famine during the 1840s. In spite of all my efforts to mask the bitter taste by adding more and more strawberry jam to the biscuits, I never liked the unfamiliar brew. At home, we drank tea from a glass, adding a Russian Swee-Touch-Nee teaball to boiling water and then lemon. For sweetening, we kept a half lump of sugar in our mouths. However, it did not take long for us to learn to use granulated sugar and to drink the tea from cups, but the rest of the ingredients remained the same.

I was always afraid of Mrs. Dart. Her dusty gray hair, bent figure, watery blue eyes, false teeth and gnarled, claw-like hands reminded me of the witches in the fairy tales I read, and I never would stay very long in her home. The sound of the dark, continually brewing tea on the stove only served to reinforce the image I had conjured up in my imagination. I realize now, of course, that this was terribly unfair. In truth, Mrs. Dart was a lonely, fragile old woman who yearned for company and who was even willing to fabricate errands to get some. As I said earlier, she was the main source of the pennies I needed to buy sweets. For going to the grocer, the reward was always a penny, except when the package was unusually heavy, which merited a two-cent tip.

Once, after I had completed an emergency errand to the drugstore and we had finished our customary tea break and I was, as usual, rushing away, she generously and impetuously presented me with a small Waterford pitcher, which she had carefully picked out from her large collection of Irish crystal on her sideboard. Foolishly, I refused the gift; all I could think of was that it would only further clutter our already cramped household.

Mr. Dart was a licensed electrician; gentle, taciturn and slightly bent over, but still robust with sparse, carefully combed white hair. Like his father before him, he was a member of Local 3 of the International Brotherhood of Electrical Workers (IBEW). Every morning, before 5:00 a.m., he left his home for work and returned by 3:00 p.m. By 3:30, he was settled at the window, which overlooked an open lot that was overgrown during the summer with weeds and wildflowers, Queen Anne's lace, sweet smelling red clover, buttercups, daisies, wild verbena and black-eyed Susans. Later, during the early fall, the deadly red sumac, goldenrod and ragweed—that bane of hayfever sufferers—merged with the foliage and added both color and congestion to the scene.

Mr. Dart would light his corncob pipe, put on his soft slippers, which were always in front of his chair, and read his paper, never saying a word. I always knew what time it was, because the acrid odor of the heavy tobacco drifted in through the open window at our end of the fire escape. Somehow, I never minded the smell; it was both reassuring and symbolic of the steady, quiet, kindly old man next door. He rarely spoke, and then only in monosyllables. I often wondered how he communicated with his wife.

Our young neighbor, Mrs. Orzeck, newly arrived from Poland, still retained the natural pink cheeks that revealed her peasant origins. Her delphinium blue eyes shone, as did her pale, blonde hair. Her plump, solidly built figure proclaimed her belief that plentiful food was the guarantee of both good health and salvation. Whenever I visited her and her cute, chubby two-year-old baby boy, Hymie, whom I enjoyed teasing, she was busy feeding him. He sat in his high chair, while she sat in front of him, stuffing cereal into his mouth and coaxing him to "*Ess, ess*" ("Eat, eat").

To Mrs. Orzeck, who had lived through starvation and the other horrors of World War I in Poland, bountiful food symbolized the American deliverance. She was determined to see to it that her family, and everyone else she liked, would be well fed.

When I was in her home, she plied me with homemade sponge cake, and, on Jewish holidays, with *gefilte* fish and hot, buttery noodle pudding, stuffed with raisins and nuts.

She always sent an extra portion for Mama, and at times, she brought some over herself.

Chapter 5
Household Geography

FIVE-AND-A-HALF OF US LIVED in four small rooms on the third floor, rear of a four-story walk-up. It had not always been thus. When Mama and Papa moved in—just before I was born—there were only four-and-a-half: Mama (pregnant), Papa, my brother, Irving and my sister, Ethel. They had selected a bright, sunshine-flooded, five-room apartment on the second floor, with southern exposure. The building had been newly built and was not yet fully occupied.

When, almost nine years later, Mama led the successful rent strike that prevented the landlord from receiving exorbitant rent increases, he decided to exact his revenge. Legally prevented from evicting us, he forced us, instead, to move into smaller quarters, claiming that he needed our old apartment for his family of three. No amount of pleading by our lawyer, who argued that five-and-a-half people, including a pregnant woman, should not be moved into smaller surroundings and required to climb an extra flight of stairs, had any effect on the judge.

Even though he was sympathetic, he still ruled that the landlord was entitled to choose any apartment he desired for himself, as long as he offered the family involved another one. To bolster his claim, the landlord contended that he needed the additional bedroom because his wife and he did not sleep together. In those days, both conjugal fealty and double beds were highly touted, and the landlord's barely audible answers produced a good deal of laughter in the courtroom. Our attorney made him repeat his answers over and over with a, "Louder please, Mr. F.—we can't hear you." (Everyone, including his wife, called him "Mr. F."). The landlord was discomfited, but it did not alter his determination to "get even." We finally had to move—piece by piece—with the help of our neighbors.

Many of the tenants felt guilty; after all, they had benefited from the strike, and the only family that had to bear the brunt of the landlord's vindictiveness was the one whose spokesperson had been largely responsible for their victory. So they readily pitched in. Three men carried up the beds, the piano, the heavy sideboard, the dining room table and chairs, the kitchen equipment, the trunk and dozens of packing boxes. The women brought up the linens, the pots and pans, our family's clothing, and an assortment of loose objects.

On the day on which we settled into our new apartment, Mrs. Reisman (second floor) baked a big chicken; Mrs. Gustafero (third floor) presented us with a large bowl of spaghetti; Mrs. Lux (second floor) delivered a salad and seeded rolls; Mrs. Berman (first floor) sent us, via her daughter, Lois, some French pastry from the German bakery across the street, and Mrs. Dart, our next door neighbor, provided a pot of genuine coffee, not chicory.

Bella Fishman, Mama's good friend, whom she had met at the Socialist Consumers League and who attended English classes with her, lived on the ground floor in the last house of the five-building complex, while ours was in the middle. The first day in the new apartment, she arrived early to clean the icebox, arranged for the iceman to deliver a 25-cent piece of ice (the largest size available for home use) and, together with Mrs. Reisman, brought up the perishable foods so they would not spoil. And in the evening, while we were eating dinner, she trooped up the stairs again bearing a hot potato pudding.

In true *major domo* style, Mama issued instructions as to where every piece of furniture should go, but there was so little space in the new surroundings that several times, the movers had to transfer a piece of furniture from one room to another. When everything was in place, we sat down for a wonderful feast after propping up the dining room table's wobbly leg with a block of wood. The fact that Irving was playing at a *bar mitzvah* made even more food and more room available for the rest of us. Since the electricity was not scheduled to be turned on until the next day, our wobbly festive table was illuminated by two candles carefully installed in brand new brass candlesticks. In the background, as we ate, the magnificent voice of Enrico Caruso resounded from the tracks of a 78rpm Victor record.

Other than room for a small, straight-backed chair near the door, the bed on which Ethel and I slept took up our entire bedroom. The one small closet in the room could not hold all our clothes. The only light room in the apartment that was intended to be the living room became, instead, the master bedroom. Its seams were bursting with a double bed, a bird's-eye maple dresser, a Singer sewing machine, two hard-backed chairs with simulated leather seats, garnered from the dining room set, a cardboard armoire, and later, to house the soon-to-be-born Donald, a crib, supplied by a friendly neighbor whose baby girl had outgrown it.

Except at night, when Irving returned late from a musical engagement and opened a folding bed, thereby transforming the room into another bedroom, the room adjoining the master bedroom served as our dining room. This was, in fact, a misnomer, since we rarely dined there and the guests for whom it was intended preferred, instead, to eat in the kitchen. The two windows set in the side wall faced east and looked directly into the apartment in the house next to ours. The so-called dining room contained the wobbly-legged table, decked out with a centerpiece of artificial fruit set into a pressed glass bowl, and a heavy, mirrored sideboard. This mahogany-stained, hardwood piece had two shelves on either side upon which rested the inexpensive knick-knacks that had accumulated through the years, the gifts brought by our neighbors, and the bric-a-brac that Papa had brought home. Our two pieces of carnival glass—a fluted bowl and a ridged flower vase—sat on the flat surface below the sideboard's mirror, together with the sky-blue frosted glass bowl Papa had once purchased impulsively, and imprudently, with his overtime pay. There were copies of Meissen figurines (a Woolworth specialty) on each side of the top shelves. On either side of the mirror, on parallel shelves, were two pseudo-Hummels: a boy and a girl. The lower section included two drawers, with their metal, leaf-designed handles, which held the silver plate cutlery (a gift from the savings bank in which Mama intermittently kept a small savings account). Beneath them, Mama placed all her bed linens, towels, two lovely linen tablecloths that Ethel had brought home from Bloomingdale's when she worked there, and an extra blanket. The upright piano, the newest and most expensive piece of furniture, stood by the wall opposite the windows. It had been purchased on credit from Krakauer Bros., "Home of Fine Pianos," whose plant and showroom stood at 136th Street and Cypress Avenue.

Mama had decided that we needed the piano when Ethel had begun piano lessons at the age of 11, insisting that she could not practice unless she had a piano in the house. It turned out that she never had time to practice, and Mama's fantasy of Ethel as a concert pianist quickly dissipated. Irving, on the other hand, learned to play the piano without any formal lessons and chose to become a jazz musician. He apparently had a good musical ear and was able to improvise the latest tunes. He and two of his schoolmates—a drummer and a bass player—formed a trio and were able to get steady work.

I never learned to play the piano—Mama became discouraged after wasting so much time and money on Ethel's lessons —but I was able to memorize the lyrics of all the popular melodies of the period. I sang along while Irving practiced, and he seldom objected, although he could well have; I could carry a tune, but my singing voice was weak and sometimes quavered. What I lacked in quality, I more than made up for in enthusiasm and feeling. I really enjoyed those sessions, intoning with passion the love-drenched lyrics.

Next to the piano stood the only comfortable chair we owned; an upholstered armchair. It was given to us by a neighbor who moved to her own home in Queens after being left a $10,000 legacy by the legendary rich uncle. She invited us to visit her so she could show off her impressive new home, but Queens seemed a million miles away, and we never did. This was poetic justice, since the armchair, reserved for guests, was rarely used.

Even the kitchen in our new apartment was smaller and we were unable to fit all of us around the kitchen table. The fact that the quarters were so cramped encouraged everyone in the family to be somewhere else at mealtimes. Irving was away most of the time, either on a job or "jamming" with friends; Ethel was always rushing—first home from work to eat and then off on a date; Papa often stayed downtown to attend a meeting. Mama tried to "hold the fort," remaining home as much as possible so we could all eat together as a family, but it was a losing battle. Still, it was the most utilized room in our home, since visitors would always join Mama even while she did her kitchen chores.

Every Saturday, I would diligently polish the dining room furniture, clambering up on the sideboard so that I could reach the high shelves or kneeling on the floor to rub the table legs. I changed the tablecloth whenever it became creased or soiled. (The two cloths we used were alike except for the color of the trim). Since we never used the tablecloths for eating, they never became really dirty. Nevertheless, I was resolved that our guest room should be shiny clean. For me, it was the one palpable evidence that, like so many of my peers, I was part of the mainstream.

It was this Saturday cleaning process that became the source of heated arguments between Irving and myself. Since he was usually sleeping, I tried to be especially quiet. However, if I dropped a figure or banged the table when the leg slipped, he would mumble, grumble and yell, "For Christ's sake, let me sleep!" Once he even threw a shoe at me. Still, stubbornly and obnoxiously, I continued.

Poor Irving! He slept directly in the path of the passing traffic to and from the master bedroom: Papa or Mama going one way, Ethel and I the other. The problem was not too serious while he was attending school and had to rise early, but it got much worse as his working hours became later and later. It remained unsolved until, after I graduated from high school, we moved to larger quarters.

Because the back room was also exposed, with only a wide doorway with a velvet portière (pulled back most of the time for light) separating it from the dining room—Mama made her bed early. She covered the sheets with a white chenille bedspread and embellished it with two multicolored crocheted pillows. During my cleaning rounds, I wiped the top of the bird's-eye dresser and shook out the cross-stitched runner before putting back the collection of cosmetics that Ethel used and kept there.

As I look back at it now, I cannot help being struck by how we were able to adapt to the changes in our living environment and to use our very limited financial resources to fashion a comfortable, livable household.

Chapter 6
A Taste of Country Living

NEITHER ETHEL NOR I EVER HAD A DOLL OF OUR OWN. I always envied my friend Lois, who owned four dolls, acquired on various celebratory occasions. Three of them lay comfortably on the pink, satin-like coverlet on Lois's bed. Mary Belle, the latest addition and the most impressive of all, had her own wicker carriage with a movable hood, which could shade the doll's eyes from the sun or shield her from the gaze of jealous children whenever Lois walked down the street.

Mary Belle was truly a sight to behold; eighteen inches tall and lifelike, with delicate porcelain face and hands. She had genuine blonde curls, deep blue eyes and long-lashed eyelids that opened and shut. When pressed tight, she would utter "Mama!" in a plaintive baby voice. She had four outfits—one for each season. Her red winter coat had its own natural rabbit skin hat and muff, which were meant to look like ermine. How overjoyed I was on the rare occasions when Lois allowed me to play with Mary Belle.

Then, just three weeks after I turned nine years old, my younger brother, Donald, was born, and I had my first opportunity to play "mother." Donald was indeed a beautiful baby; he, too, had blond curls, blue eyes and a soft, rosebud mouth. He was gurgly and cheerful and fun to dress and feed. When Mama stopped breast feeding him at one year, I took over some of her chores. I would proudly wheel his carriage down the block and back again. I gloated visibly when neighbors, and sometimes total strangers, peered into the pram and exclaimed enthusiastically about how he looked, insisting that he was so pretty, he must be a girl.

Since Donald provided much more satisfaction than Mary Belle, I soon got over my jealousy. He laughed; he hugged me; he clutched my fingers; he cried; before he was a year old, he was already saying, "Papa"; at 15 months, he was already walking: and he would respond with appreciative sounds when I talked or read to him. And best of all, it was not long before Lois was vying for the privilege of pushing his carriage and offering me Mary Belle any time I desired. I noted with pleasure how infrequently I wanted to make the exchange.

It was during her pregnancy that Mama told me how babies were "made." Of course, I had already been privy to such street gossip as "I saw," "I heard," "Sidney said," "they did"—but I knew it couldn't be true.

Mama, who was never really thin, remained Rubenesque after my birth. She wore tight corsets and pulled the strings very tight to contain her figure and to provide a visible waist below her full breasts. As her pregnancy progressed, however, she became heavier and heavier, and I became more and more insistent in demanding why she didn't wear her corset. One day, while she was washing my hair, I turned, pushed her roughly and said, "You're so fat, you're bumping me, Mama! Why don't you pull in your stomach?" I had pushed her so hard that she almost cried. Instead, she told me the proverbial "facts of life." I was shocked, overwhelmed, disbelieving and completely bewildered—all of the above—but over the next three months, before the baby arrived, I was both helpful and solicitous. Mama, meanwhile, comforted me by letting me listen to the fetus moving within her.

Just before Donald was born, Mama made a momentous decision. Torn between the pride she felt in her luxurious, warm brown hair, which she wore piled high on her head, and the desire to make a statement, she decided to join the large body of women who were asserting their emancipation by cutting their hair. When one of her best friends, Mrs. Plotnick, returned from the beauty parlor attractive but shorn, Mama took the plunge. In a traumatic reversal of roles, she grasped my hand for reassurance and marched to the beauty parlor halfway down the block. A half hour later, she emerged a little sad, but relieved and triumphant. She was clutching my hand for reassurance and holding the foot-and-a-half braid of coiled hair in her other palm. Papa wasn't quite sure he approved of the change. Mama did look different—younger—but still different. After some mild remonstrance, he finally accepted it as just one more of Mama's long list of statements of independence. I wasn't sure I liked it, either, but I said nothing, sensing Mama's tension over the subject. I remember sitting opposite the barber's chair, watching the scissors irrevocably snip the long, thick hair that looked almost alive as it fell into the barber's hands. I wanted to cry—and, in fact, I think I actually did—but Mama was too concerned, anxiously watching the barber, to notice me.

While these earth-shaking events were taking place at home, Papa was fully occupied with the struggle for better conditions in the garment center and with the bitter internecine conflict between the "left" and "right" in the union. I sometimes accompanied Mama to the many meetings, demonstrations, picket lines and marches in which the housewives showed a heightened degree of militancy. I also marched with Mama for women's suffrage before it was finally won in 1920, helped her picket stores that were charging exorbitant prices, accompanied her on her meetings with frustrated tenants, and listened as she spoke out against abuses of civil rights and liberties. I particularly liked the suffrage events: the women looked so well in their shirtwaists, long skirts and elaborate hats.

I also regularly wheeled Donald's carriage down Cypress Avenue to 143rd Street and St. Mary's Park. I pushed him on the baby swings or sat behind him on one end of the seesaw while another child provided balance on the other end. Donald loved the activities in the park. As he grew older, he played with other children in the sandbox, building sand castles and tunnels with his pail and shovel. One day, when he was about two years old, he begged me to let him try the glide down the sliding pond. Since most of the children sliding down the pond were older, I was afraid to trust him alone on it. He was persistent, however, and began to wail. Finally, I went up with him, holding his hand as he climbed the stairs. His progress was slow, and the children behind us became impatient. To hasten the process, I grabbed him as we reached the top step and started to go over the top. I was still not fast enough for those behind me, and someone gave me a shove. I lost my footing and down I tumbled over the slide, still holding fast to Donald. Fortunately, he fell on top of me as I toppled, face down. Someone screamed—perhaps it was I—and after what seemed hours but was actually less than a minute, a bunch of scared kids picked me up, placed a crying Donald into his carriage and sat me down on a nearby bench. Some adults who had accompanied their children to the park came over to soothe my sobbing brother, who was frightened but unhurt. They then turned to assess the damage I had sustained. I was slightly dazed and shaken, but I was able to walk. My right wrist bone was definitely protruding unnaturally and it hurt very badly.

I rested for a while, refused further offers of help, and, using my left hand, propelled the carriage to Lincoln Hospital just a few blocks away. The doctor in the Emergency Room diagnosed a broken wrist, swiftly set it and put my arm in a cast and a sling. He then checked the now quiet Donald for cuts and bruises—miraculously there were none—and sent us on our way. We left; Donald with a dirty face that was slightly swollen from crying, and me with a fresh, cumbersome plastic dressing and much less pain. During the month in which I wore the cast, we made no trips to the park, but as soon as it came off, Donald demanded that we go back. We did, but we did not attempt the sliding pond until Donald was able to negotiate it on his own.

THERE WERE OTHER NOTABLE EVENTS that summer of 1924. I saw, then milked my first cow; patted, then rode my first (and last) horse and spent two weeks in the lush, green surroundings and the exhilarating fresh air of the mountainous state of Vermont.

Mama had registered me at the Fresh Air Fund of Lincoln Hospital, established for children whose parents could not afford to send them to camp for the summer. People in outlying rural areas opened up their houses and hospitality to from one to a dozen youngsters, usually for a fortnight, so that these children could enjoy the pleasures and duties of farm living. I was given a departure date in the middle of August, the last trip of the season. It was about a month after my accident and the cast had been removed. There were about 90 children assembled in the two buses that left that August day; one bound for Pennsylvania and ours for Vermont. For most of us, it was the first time away from our families. Despite the general sense of anticipation and excitement, there were a few tearful parting scenes. Two of the children refused to go, even after their mothers had forcibly thrust them into their seats. We left without them, gulping down our own fears. We had no encouraging hand to grip as we departed.

Mr. and Mrs. Bradford were a childless couple who owned a medium-sized farm in St. Johnsbury in northern Vermont, not far from the Canadian border. Their home was surrounded by verdant hills. They had a dozen well-fed cows, three dozen noisy chickens, two mongrel dogs named Vernon and Spotty, and a sedate, even-tempered aging horse they called Bessie, who earned her keep by helping with the spring plowing. During the rest of the year, she moved about the farm with all the authority of a co-owner, surveying the general activity with approval, watching the growing corn, overseeing the vegetable garden and graciously accepting the gentle stroking of her back by the ever-present well-wishers. She often accompanied us—the two children who were guests—as we helped with the chores and even allowed us to ride her bareback.

Nora and I had met each other for the first time on the bus to Vermont. We each had our own room—a pure, undiluted pleasure neither of us had ever experienced before. Mine had a single bed, with a fancy, metal, gold-painted headboard, at the center of which was a cherubic angel with a bright smile and short, spread wings. There was also an oak dresser of indeterminate age and style, with three commodious drawers, and an oak framed round mirror attached to the dresser by curved oak strips. A straight-backed chair with a worn yellow silk seat, and a closet, set on the wall, with two lower drawers for miscellaneous socks and handkerchiefs, completed the furnishings. The window, framed with a yellow, lace curtain, looked out on the vegetable garden, where tomatoes, string beans and squash were ripening. It not only looked like heaven, but the smell of new-mown hay made it smell like heaven, too. On those nights when Nora and I were not too tired after supper, we would exchange tales of our experiences that day.

Nora and I were taught to visit the chicken coops every morning to gather fresh eggs in our baskets without disturbing the clucking hens. Each day, we compared our collections, and the one who had picked the greatest number by the end of the week was declared the winner. Since Nora won the first week and I the second, we had to draw lots to determine who would sit by the window on the bus on the way home.

Every cow had a name, and on the third day, I learned to milk Rachel. I milked her every day in the late afternoon, after we had gone with Mr. Bradford to drive the cows home. Nora milked Nancy. When we finished our work, we each had a cup of the fresh, warm, foamy milk, and Mrs. Bradford brought us corn or blueberry muffins, just out of the oven, to help us adapt to the strange taste.

Mrs. Bradford was a kind-hearted, middle-aged, buxom woman with graying hair pulled back in a tight bun. As she bent over her work, single strands, which she pushed back impatiently, continuously escaped. She greeted us affectionately every morning and kissed us at night before we went upstairs to bed. She fed us well with fresh food, almost all of which she and her husband grew or produced on the farm. We had ham and eggs for breakfast, washed down with two huge glasses of milk; fresh cheese sandwiches on homemade bread for lunch; corn or blueberry muffins with our milk at milking time, and for supper, thick vegetable soups and roast chicken or beef with boiled or baked potatoes. For dessert, there was always a freshly baked pie—apple, blackberry or sweet potato.

On the first Saturday after our arrival, Mrs. Bradford took us on a picnic, where we had cold chicken, newly picked tomatoes, fresh corn and pie. Mr. Bradford remained at home to take care of his afternoon chores and read his weekly newspaper. After-ward, Nora and I climbed a tall, hilly knoll about a mile from the house and marveled at the view of the unbroken stretch of green, cultivated fields below and the long line of gently rounded mountains above. It was a perfect day and left us totally unpre-pared for what happened next.

When we returned home at about 3:00 p.m., there was a del-egation of fifteen people waiting for us—five children, ranging in age from five to fifteen, four men and six women. They had heard there was a Jew at the Bradfords, and never having seen one, they were curious to see what I looked like. Would I, they must have wondered, have horns—even small ones—growing out of my head? We learned later that they had arrived about a half hour before we did and that Mr. Bradford had spent the entire time trying to convince them, first politely, then more firmly, that they should leave; that there was nothing to see.

I think they were disappointed and embarrassed when they were unable to tell which of us, Nora or I, was the "freak." Nora was a pretty Irish girl with penetrating brown eyes, short blonde hair and a pleasant grin. The visitors stared at me unblinkingly, then someone, probably one of the two boys from town who sometimes helped Mr. Bradford with the farm work, pointed me out to them. I stared back at them—even as I am staring now at the four photographs that remain as souvenirs of the brief sojourn in Vermont that summer. I see a tall, gangly, somewhat solemn-looking kid of eleven. I was five feet, three inches tall —a height I never exceeded—just about Mrs. Bradford's size and a head taller than Nora, with brown hair shading into auburn, cut in the Buster Brown style. My eyes, too, were deep brown, large and expressive, my nose Greek-straight, and my smile, to my eyes, infectious. I could well have been the Irish one and Nora the Jew.

Finally, one of the men spoke, sounding frustrated: "But she doesn't look different." "I'm not different," I replied angrily. "Why should I be?" No one could give an answer until the oldest boy said, "She sounds different, though. She doesn't speak like us."

His mother reminded him that everyone who came from New York spoke that way.

After apologizing for their rudeness, they returned to St. Johnsbury, from whence they had come. When they left, I broke into tears, sobbing. Both Mr. and Mrs. Bradford comforted me, patting me gently, and telling me that I should pay no attention to these people; that they were just plain ignorant.

Part III
Out in the World

Chapter 7
A Rare Learning Experience

WE WERE 30 STUDENTS in a special experimental class for the gifted, organized in September, 1926, at Walton, an all-girls high school in the South Bronx. Walton's citywide reputation for quality education had enabled its principal, Miss Mary Conlin, to convince the New York City Board of Education to establish this pilot program. Its purpose was to place the brightest students in classes conducted by the finest teachers, most of them heads of their respective departments. This group would continue together, from class to class and from grade to grade, with the same instructors, for their full three years of senior high school studies. Innovative? It certainly was. Miss Conlin thought so. She had persuaded the powers that were to approve it and she guided it personally.

We were a disparate but oddly homogeneous group, most of us children of blue collar immigrants whose forebears had lived in Eastern Europe, Ireland and Italy. Many of us resided in the working class neighborhood in which Walton was located, but others came from the wealthier West Bronx. Otile Hickey's father was a construction worker; Mary Gustafero's father an iceman; mine a garment worker; but the father of my best friend in the class was different—he was an insurance agent. Myrtle Abraham and her brother and parents lived on Townsend Avenue, in the West Bronx. Her parents, and theirs before them, had been born in New York City. To me, the most surprising thing about them was that, unlike all our neighbors, they spoke English without a foreign accent, and Mr. Abraham had actually gone to high school, just as we did.

Our teachers, both male and female, were inspired to make the program work. They planned their curricula carefully so as to engage our interest and to ensure our wholehearted participation. This did not prove to be too difficult. We were an intensely motivated group, eagerly absorbing the concepts set forth by our mentors, always questioning and turning each session into a veritable feast of new information, like newborn birds hungrily swallowing the worms of knowledge.

I remember the names and physical appearances of all these remarkable people. Perhaps the memory persists because we worked together several times a week for three years, but I am sure it also remains because each of us gave so much to the entire group. In short, we all cared! As for the teachers, there was Mrs. Feier, our English teacher of 40-plus years; short, buxom, simply yet elegantly dressed, with a stern manner that tolerated no waste of time, simply because time was so limited and there was so much to learn. She succeeded in transforming the otherwise dreary and tedious grammar lessons into a fascinating journey during which we discovered new words, learned how to spell them correctly, and were able to parse the verbs so that we automatically used the correct tense.

She made each class a source of greater fluidity in our use of English. I learned the meaning (and spelling) of words like "ubiquitous," "vicissitude" and "mellifluous," and I never forgot them. And when I grandly misused the word "beget" to describe the woman's function, I learned, red-faced, that it was the man's role.

Mrs. Feier also taught me humility when, as a 13-year-old adolescent, I proudly answered "Miss Epstein," when she asked for our names during the first roll call. No lady says that, she informed me, and, to this day, I introduce myself as "Dorothy Epstein," shunning the antecedent "Miss." I attribute my abiding interest in the nuances of language, my continuing concern for the use of good grammar, my infatuation with words and my passion for literature all to this exceptional woman.

I fell in love with Mr. Corbett, our math teacher, who was the spitting image of Leslie Howard, the popular British movie star. Tall, thin, blond, with an inordinately high forehead, he even had a British accent. But more impressive than his appearance or diction was his ability to make sense of the letters, the numbers, the angles and the equations that are the bane of many a math student's existence. As we moved on to advanced algebra and geometry, the equations continued, mysteriously but logically, to reach the proper conclusions. I experienced the elation of pursuing a problem through to its correct solution.

Then there was Miss Obear, the big, dour Scottish Presbyterian, with magnificent copper-glinted hair, who was the faculty advisor to our drama club and to the Senior Arista honor society. She rarely smiled, and the girls all feared her strict discipline, but when, on opening night at Town Hall, where we were performing *The Thrice-Promised Bride*, I was literally pushed into the spotlight to play the principal role of the Magistrate, because the regular actress was ill and her understudy absent, Miss Obear kissed me after it was over and after the loud applause had subsided. In my senior class book, she wrote, "My congratulations to the heroine of *The Thrice-Promised Bride*," and she sent me a note instructing me that when the yearbook photographer came, I was to pose in the magistrate's robe and not in the costume for the small part I usually played. I don't have the pictures, but I still have the note.

William Hamm, our social studies teacher, six-foot-two, solid, ruddy-faced and ever cheerful, was the most relaxed of the faculty group, but to me the most inspiring. History came alive as he narrated the dates and events in the context of their political and social milieus. In his soft, slurred, southern English, the French Revolution became a vivid history of that country's people. His specialty was American history, and he had written several respected textbooks on that subject. He held me in thrall with his passionate reading of the speeches and writings of Jefferson, Paine and Franklin, conveying their strength and convictions, as well as their agony. Because I wanted to learn more about them, I determined then and there to become a history major in college.

Young, stylish and dynamic Rose Kurz taught us French by speaking only that language in class. Our music teacher, Miss Schein, conducted our glee club and introduced us to the musical classics. And there were many more!

Our enthusiasm and energy spilled over into our after-school activities. The school remained open until 5:00 p.m. every day. We wrote for the school paper (I was the senior class editor); formed clubs with creative and imaginative names – the history club was called *Clio*, after the Muse; the math club, *Hypatia*, for the wise and lovely Egyptian woman scholar, and we called the club we formed for our group *Quid Nunc* ("What now?"). I played basketball on the team that won many interscholastic games and participated in student government, where we conducted serious election campaigns, with slogans, posters, debates, and even campaign managers!

When I ran for president of the senior class, I was able to polish my oratorical skills. When I lost by two votes, I was deeply upset. I had worked hard and my campaign manager had prepared posters and made speeches on my behalf. I determined that next time, I would work even harder and make all my own presentations. During that period, I was elected president of the Senior Arista, a position that required no special campaign skills.

Not surprisingly, our group received most of the honors at graduation, and about 90% of us went on to college. Most, of course, went to Hunter, which was tuition-free. Some of us, myself included, were helped by a four-year scholarship stipend of $100 per year. My very good friend Virginia Lubkin matriculated at New York University and Rita Cooke at Vassar, but they were the exceptions. Those of us who could not afford college went on to secretarial school.

The seeds of intellectual curiosity, motivation and fierce determination, carefully nurtured by our parents, teachers and the community, reaped a bountiful harvest. Many of us became professionals and leaders who transcended the limits of poverty, gender and minority status. We were the children of the striving, upwardly mobile, idealistic immigrants of that era.

The all-girl high school graduation class of '29 later became the college graduating class of '33, which produced teachers, social workers, labor leaders, doctors and economists. For example, Virginia became a highly respected ophthalmologist; Ann Spiegel moved on to become an important research statistician at the United States Treasury Department.

Myrtle Abraham and I had bonded on our very first day at school. It was while signing up for courses that we discovered that we were to be fellow students in the pilot program. We were both excited at the prospect of participating in a special class with what we had heard were the best teachers at Walton. Myrtle was about two inches shorter than I, slightly rounder in build and with a young, open face, wide blue eyes, a snub nose and full, well-shaped lips. She was both generous and self-confident. Coming, as she did, from a financially comfortable family and with parents born in this country, she did not have the insecurity that beset so many of the rest of us—children of the new immigrants. Myrtle and I spent a good deal of time together at school. We made sure to meet regularly for lunch, for after-school activities and for social pursuits during our free time.

It did not take long for me to be invited for Friday night dinner at the Abrahams—"dinner," not " supper," as we called it at home. Myrtle's mother taught me to set the table properly, using real silver flatware and a Bavarian china set she had inherited from her mother. I recall that the pattern had an attractive border of small, pink roses and pale green leaves. There were also crystal wine goblets. Myrtle assured me that these were their customary tableware.

On one occasion, when her parents went out after dinner, Myrtle invited me to spend the night. She had her own room and a nice, wide bed. I was able to reach Mama through the Lux telephone belonging to a lower-floor neighbor, and she agreed to my stay-over. Myrtle and I talked and talked through half the night, each revealing our hopes and dreams, recounting episodes we had not shared with anyone else, confessing our "crushes," discussing boys, what we were reading, and then boys again. We were 13, and we remained best friends until high school graduation. We went to Hunter together, but by then, conditions had changed drastically. Our country was deep into the Great Depression. We followed completely different academic programs. Myrtle was a psychology major. Then, in the middle of our freshman year, through an introduction engineered by one of her numerous cousins, she met her future husband. Her focus changed completely. At her parents' insistence, she reluctantly went on to graduate from college and married soon after. She had long ago confided in me that her main ambition, like that of so many other young women, had been to meet a wonderful guy, marry him and have lots of beautiful children. In the letters we exchanged after she had moved to the Midwest, it appeared that her dream was fulfilled.

On many occasions during the time we spent together, Myrtle and I would meet classmates at one of the new art deco, opulent movie houses that then graced the Times Square area. On Saturday mornings, we could get a seat in the balcony for 35 cents, see a first-run movie and then gape to our hearts' content at the ornate furnishings, the high, decorated ceiling, the dazzling chandeliers, the rich, red rugs and the sumptuous lobby. There was the Capitol Theatre, built in 1919, the Roxy and Paramount built in the '20s, and, then, after we had gone on to Hunter College, there was Radio City Music Hall, built in 1932 at the height (or in the depths) of the depression. We used to gaze in awe at the lines of patrons that stretched around the block, waiting to get into the largest and most magnificent theater in the world.

When we were about to graduate from high school at sixteen—like me, Myrtle was a Gemini and was born three days before I was—her mother planned and paid for a special "Sweet Sixteen" party for five couples and arranged for Myrtle's cousin, Milton, to be my escort and his friend to be Myrtle's. I ate my first meal in a Chinese restaurant on West 34th Street and attended my first Broadway musical, *New Moon*. Our young escorts bought us gardenias, which we wore on our wrists. I can still sing some of the songs from the show, with all their lyrics.

Mrs. Abraham, my height, slender and always modestly though carefully dressed, was very observant and expressed a great deal of interest in our progress at school. She always asked me about my studies when I visited their home. That summer, I was invited to spend a week at their family's rented cottage in Far Rockaway.

A week after Myrtle's Sweet Sixteen party, Mama approached me and said: "How would you like to celebrate your birthday and your graduation from high school by a week in the country with some of the family? We can even ask Myrtle—it'll be good to take *her* out for a change."

"Mama," I replied. "Why do you ask? You know we can't afford it. Are you teasing me?" But Mama was serious. She had pulled a magic trick out of a sock! Knowing that my graduation was imminent and that I was her first child to complete high school, and aware that we owed reciprocal generosity to my best friend, Mama had saved the small change left over from shopping for over a year.

We went to Camp Unity in Wingdale, New York for a week, at a special rate, Mama, Donald and I. Papa came up for the weekend. Although Myrtle couldn't make it (she was devastated), her cousin, Milton, could.

We all really enjoyed the change, even though I brought back a badly-set pinky, victim of a poorly received medicine ball thrown by a new friend. Also, I developed a deep love for Sholem Aleichem, the popular Jewish writer. Yuri Suhl, a young immigrant writer from Poland, read us a new story every day after lunch. I developed a strong taste for Yiddish, with its dry humor, and for Sholem Aleichem in particular.

That was a happy time!

WHENEVER I HEAR THE DEBATE, which still crops up from time to time, on whether or not it is helpful to have high schools and colleges separated by gender, I think of my own experiences. I attended an all-girls high school and a women's college and found them both conducive to learning and to working with my peers, without having to deal with gender competition. Also, in both faculty and student bodies, women were in positions of leadership, and this gave us confidence in our own ability to take command. We did not feel compelled to accept any jobs offered us that did not meet the high standards we had set for ourselves. In fact, I consciously determined not to become proficient in stenography and typewriting so that I would not be swept, as so many educated women have been, into a secretarial job, doing the essential clerical work instead of the type of creative position that I was seeking.

There is, however, a negative for which I was only partially prepared, and that was facing a world in which it was an accepted fact that men were superior. From my earliest post-college jobs, I held positions in which most of my associates were men. I found out that there was a glass ceiling, that wages were disproportionate by sex, and that, all too often, women were treated with a patronizing attitude by their male peers. Despite these handicaps, and largely because I determined to ignore them, I managed, through hard work and persistence, to move ahead. Much of this preceded the growth of the feminist movement in the '60s, but even now, almost half a century after the publication of Betty Friedan's *Feminine Mystique*, there are still many problems of inequality of the sexes. We have never, for example, had either a female president or vice-president, female CEOs of major companies are still rarities, and, in the trade union field that has been an important part of my life, I know of only one female national union president.

Women still receive only 77% of men's wages for equivalent work, hold only 14% of the seats in both houses of Congress, 23% of those in state legislatures and only one-third of the seats in New York's City Council. For only the first time in our history, today there is a woman minority leader in the House of Representatives. In 1933, the same year in which I graduated from college, Franklin D. Roosevelt became the first president astute enough to appoint a woman to a cabinet post—Frances Perkins as Secretary of Labor. Then there was a long hiatus before our country's two most recent presidents, Bill Clinton, who chose Madeline K. Albright, and George W. Bush, who selected Condoleezza Rice—both named women to fill the most important post in their cabinet—that of Secretary of State.

On the other side of the ledger, 70% of the world's 1.3 billion poor are women, as are 66% of the world's one billion illiterate persons, while a full 80% of all refugees and displaced persons, globally, are women and children.

Economically, politically and socially, we still have a long way to go, baby!

Chapter 8
Hunter College: 1929-1933

KLANG! KLONG! KLANG! rang the hundreds of heels—high, low, medium, wooden, and metal-tipped—followed by a deeper, reverberating echo. They resounded on the metal steps of the commercial building at 145 East 32nd Street in Manhattan in which Hunter College had leased four floors. Because of heavy registration and severe over-crowding at the college's main location at 68th Street and Lexington Avenue, that was where I spent much of my first two years at college. We were continuously moving from room to room as we changed classes. We went up and down and down and up, our shrill young voices raised to a high volume in order to drown out the other noises. Sometimes, a heel got caught in the openwork of a stair, and the whole line slowed down until the shoe, and its owner, could move again.

The constant din and the dull, unembellished battleship-gray walls in the halls and rooms where we assembled to study and learn seemed to symbolize both the difficult times we were going through and our strong, persevering efforts to complete our studies in spite of them. But the utilitarian walls in each room also sheltered us from the chaos outside, leaving us free to ingest huge chunks of knowledge that would be indispensable in our future life work.

I came to Hunter in September, 1929. Just one month later—in October—the tragic stock market crash precipitated a major catastrophe in the country. Many of our fathers, along with many of our older brothers and sisters, lost their jobs—or else they had to work for half their former wage. Some of my classmates were forced to drop out of school; they simply could not afford to continue their studies. We awoke every day to a combination of personal difficulties and headlines proclaiming in enormous type the suicide of another formerly rich individual rendered penniless by the market disaster.

I had been thrilled by my acceptance at Hunter. Unlike so many others of my contemporaries who longed to go away to more prestigious schools, I was only too glad to remain in New

York, at a school with high standards and one that provided—for the students who worked hard—an education without tuition, and with free books and excellent teachers. For me, there was the added opportunity of continuing my education while still enjoying the companionship of some of my good friends from high school.

Our instructors had to teach under the most difficult circumstances. All of them had been affected, in one way or another, by the economic disaster that had stunned the nation. In addition, they had to handle teenagers who were also experiencing great stress. However, they were consoled by the knowledge that these young students, despite the hardships they were experiencing, were earnestly determined to complete their studies.

The teachers I remember were not necessarily my best ones, but rather those who tried to make their classes as stimulating and inviting as possible. There was Professor MacLear, who lectured on medieval history and who had been at the school for many years—35 when she retired. She had straight, graying hair pulled back into a tight bun and a sharp-featured face with piercing eyes. She wore the same rusty wool dress day after day. When she described the feudal system, with its serfs and guilds, she looked like a woman of the period come alive to help bring it back to life. She lived a short distance from the main Hunter building, in a dark, six-room railroad flat, with several cats in every room—meowing, fighting, playing and moving. When she heard that I had grown up in a household with cats, she invited me over. As we walked down the long hall, the caterwauling became louder and the strong, sharp odor of cat urine became overwhelming. Fortunately, we did not stay long. Professor MacLear picked up a handsome alley cat with a bell around its neck and said, "Here's Jingles. He's one of my best cats. I know you'll love him." Since our own wonderful cat, Patty, had died recently, Mama welcomed the new arrival enthusiastically, and Jingles joined the family.

Miss Etta Schreiber, my instructor in German, taught us the declension of difficult verbs in song. I recall three of them:

Heinrich Heine's *Heiden Roslein, Die Lorelei* and an idiotic song about a hat. Whenever I am troubled, I sing the hat melody. It goes: *Mein hut es hät drei ecken. Drei ecken hät mein hut. Und hät es nicht drei ecken. So war es nicht mein hut.* ("My hat, it has three corners. Three corners has my hat. And had it not three corners, it would not be my hat"). Miss Schreiber was always cheerful, greeting us with a "homey" smile. I was pleased to learn from the Hunter archivist that she was his German teacher when he matriculated at Hunter 20 years after I did.

Miss Goldstein, a tall, attractive young physiology teacher, had an exciting new point to make each time we came to class. She treated us all as if we were indispensable to the success of the class, which made attendance a pleasure.

Of course, I missed having a green campus and trees under which to sit when the weather was fair, with bright yellow forsythia, flaming azaleas and other flowering shrubs, while the birds sang above, but I still felt fortunate that I was attending an excellent college close to home. And to make matters even better, that first year I worked on Saturdays in the flower shop at Bloomingdale's department store for the munificent sum of three dollars per day. I sold and carefully wrapped the lovely blossoms whose names I had mastered and whose scents, some rich and almost overpowering, I learned to associate with the names of the flowers that exuded them. There were, of course, roses, whose long stems reached the end of the box that held them—plus anemones, freesia, delphinium, lilies of the valley, orchids, gardenias (for corsages), calceolaria, cineraria, calla lilies and lilacs. Because I enjoyed the experience so much, I can still identify most of these intoxicating blooms, which surprises a lot of people. They should know how easy it is when one works selling flowers every Saturday for a year.

I had decided that, unlike high school, where I had participated extensively in extracurricular activities, at Hunter I would concentrate on my studies in order to learn everything I could. I would assiduously avoid any activities that would divert me from that goal. I not only felt an obligation to my family for their sacrifices for my education—they had firmly answered "No" when I offered to get a full-time job in order to help out—but it also satisfied my desire to concentrate on acquiring all the knowledge I could in an atmosphere created for just that purpose. When again, I asked myself, would I have such an opportunity?

I also carried out another high school decision when I made history my major. I was joined in this choice by two of my good friends from Walton, Lillian Mittman and Rebecca Sobin. We compared notes and exchanged opinions, arguing animatedly about our respective conclusions. Some of our peers would join in these heated discussions. Unfortunately, these opportunities were necessarily infrequent, since many of us worked after school and had other concerns, including the need to prepare daily for the next day's classes.

ADDED TO ALL THIS WAS MY FAMILY'S TASK of looking for a new apartment. We seemed to be constantly packing and unpacking, moving into or out of one apartment or another. We all had ambivalent feelings about moving from our 138th Street home. Mama had been engaged in a wide range of activities during which she had made so many friends that the prospect of leaving was one that neither she nor the rest of us welcomed. In addition, I had lived there since I was born. Ethel and Irving, too, had many ties to the community that would be hard to duplicate elsewhere.

On the other hand, the apartment we had lived in for the past nine years was gloomy and small enough to induce claustrophobia. Our family had expanded since we had moved there and we kept literally bumping into each other. Besides, better, bigger and brighter apartments had now become available elsewhere at lower rent. Secure in the knowledge that we could still return to visit our old friends, we rented a large, five-room, fifth floor walk-up apartment in a building at the corner of Elsmere Place and Southern Boulevard in the East Bronx. The rooms were bright and airy, with south and east exposure and all windows facing the street. And we had so much more room!

Mama had just finished paying for our upright piano. Even though Ethel had not fulfilled Mama's dream that she become a concert pianist, she still enjoyed playing on occasion, and Irving still practiced his jazz. As for me, I was just glad that we had moved to a place where more than one person could stand near the piano and join in the singing without having to constantly step out of the way to let someone pass.

However, moving the piano was not so simple. It had to be layered in heavy felt, tied with sturdy rope and lowered by pulley gently to the ground, *via* an outside window. It took a total of four men to complete the operation—two in the apartment guiding its movements and yelling to the other two down below, who shouted back "A little to the left," or "Watch out for the big plant on the window ledge on the second floor!" All told, moving the piano more than doubled the basic moving charges. As a result, when we had to move from Elsmere Place a year and a half later because we had to find a cheaper apartment, we left the piano behind. Mama announced this momentous decision after spending two sleepless nights. She had reluctantly come to the conclusion that, as our income dropped, we would have to be constantly moving from one place to another. Under those circumstances, the cost of constantly moving the piano far exceeded the benefits we derived from it.

We cried when she announced her decision and I clung tightly to her. Of course, the piano looked particularly attractive from the polishing I had just given it. Mama smiled ruefully as she said, "Ethel doesn't play much any more and Irving can easily find another place to practice. If it's any comfort to you, this is happening all over the city to hundreds of other families—maybe even thousands—who have to relocate to lower-rent apartments." And she was right. So many parents' dreams of fame for their children were being literally destroyed—shattered because their pianos were being chopped up into firewood.

"Perhaps," Mama went on, "the next occupants will love and enjoy such a fine piano. It does look so good! And maybe we'll be lucky enough to find a piano after we move. Nobody seems to be able to find a customer for their pianos—not even to give it away, free. The only pianos that can be sold today are the baby grands with the Jewish name" (she meant, of course, Steinway).

As moving became a regular part of our lives, we had to factor moving expenses into our family budget. We realized that we had to get rid of some of our possessions in order to keep bringing down our moving costs. Of course, the other side of the equation was keeping what was necessary for the household since we had no money with which to purchase replacements. One item in the first category became old phonograph records, and many one-time precious recordings landed in the garbage. My younger brother, Donald, as the only sibling available for the purpose, was called upon to play an important role in the moving process.

Recently, while the two of us were exchanging reminiscences about the period, I asked him if there were any incidents he considered noteworthy. "Yes," he answered regretfully, "I was perhaps a little too enthusiastic about eliminating whatever was possible from the items we packed. It seemed natural to me that we should discard our Caruso records. They hadn't been played since I was five or six. So, during one of the packing experiences, when I was about 10 years old, I dumped them. After the move was completed, I casually reported what I had done to Mama and Papa. Papa blanched and said nothing, but left the room. He never chastised me—never mentioned it, but I remember it because he looked so upset." Don had not even been born when our parents starting accumulating their Caruso collection and he knew nothing of its history. When I told him the background, he was horrified.

Sunday, for me, was library day, when I went down to the main library at 42nd Street and Fifth Avenue to do research. I loved the smell of the rich, leather bindings which denoted books that were old and full of classical tradition. I particularly liked the soothing atmosphere at the library and the efficient, helpful advisers, along with the individual desks, the soft lights and the quiet—and everywhere, the heads bent over piles of books. There were also the many alluring side rooms with their changing exhibits mounted in polished mahogany-framed glass cases, which I was able to visit and enjoy if I finished my work early enough.

Even though it was a shorter trip to enter the building through the side door near the elevators, I would come in through the front entrance as often as I could whenever I was not pressed for time. I admired the two massive, benevolent looking lions guarding the entrance—still performing that duty today after almost a century—the sweep of the stairs and the elegance of the main foyer, with its high, vaulted ceiling and its intricate plaster work. It had all been so beautifully conceived and executed by Carrère and Hastings, prominent architects in 1911, when it was built. The fact that I could utilize this magnificent building and its priceless treasures was a constant source of deep gratification for me.

I took many notes in my various loose-leaf books, particularly for my history and political science courses. I was developing research skills that were to stand me in good stead in the years that followed, whatever the activity in which I was engaged.

When we attended classes in the neo-Gothic building on Park Avenue between East 68th and 69th Streets, during our junior and senior years, I felt more at ease: we were in our "home" building. On warm days, we were able to use Central Park (situated two blocks away) as our campus, enjoying our lunch on the grass and lingering there when we had no afternoon classes. Once or twice, we even played "hookey!"

There were 764 proud graduates of the Class of '33 at the commencement exercises held at Carnegie Hall on Wednesday morning, June 14, 1933. My history classmate, Mildred Perlman, had earned her degree over five-and-a-half years, attending evening session. Another, Ray Beinhacher, who, along with me and 40 other graduates, made the Phi Beta Kappa honor society, had almost quit school during the first year. Our indefatigable energy, our hopes, our determination and our aspirations for the future had kept us together under the most difficult circumstances.

ONE EVENING, just about a month before graduation, I saw Papa and Mama in the kitchen, having an animated, low-pitched conversation in Russian. Their use of Russian told me that what they were talking about was important, and I also knew from the quiet manner in which they were expressing themselves that their discussion was amicable. After they had been talking for about 15 minutes, I walked past the kitchen and Mama called me in. They were both smiling broadly, although I noted that Mama's smile was somewhat rueful. She began by conceding that in this instance, at least, Papa was right.

"There are times," she went on, "when we can allow ourselves to think of something besides the bills that have to be paid, and now is such a time. How would you like to go to see the Chicago World's Fair and at the same time visit with your aunts, uncles and cousins? After all, what you have accomplished, Dorothy, has a world of importance. You are the first daughter of all the sisters in this country to graduate from college. The boys have grown up to be a doctor, dentists, an engineer and a pharmacist —but the girls are all secretaries, except two who went to normal school to become teachers. We're very proud of you. Papa and I want to show you off to Aunt Pearl, Aunt Anna and their families. We'll do it somehow!"

It was evident to me that in those distressing, trouble-filled times, this was very important to them, and I could well understand why. Mama was eager to show her sisters, who were a little better off, that her daughter had taken a major step forward in her education.

And so, Mama, Donald and I took the train to Chicago. Anna's daughter, Sarah and Pearl's daughter, Suzanne were two or three years older than I. We spent the days visiting the many 1933 World's Fair art deco buildings and getting a sense of what the future might hold in store for us. The exhibits depicted both technical and architectural developments. We also found time to go to the beach, the movies and several restaurants, and, of course, to the famous Marshall Field's department store.

Aunt Minnie came in from San Francisco to join her siblings for a reunion of the sisters—the first time they had been together since leaving Russia. All of them were present except Mary, who sent a message of greetings and good wishes from Minsk. Minnie, Pearl and Anna gave Mama a handsome check to cover our travel expenses and more. (Somehow, I think that immediately after we decided to make the trip, Mama made sure that this was going to happen. She was still very much concerned about the economic problems we faced in the period ahead and could only see her way clear to making the trip if we were able to obtain that kind of help.)

Regardless of these worries, the events in Chicago were an extraordinary experience and I enjoyed every minute of it.

Part IV
The Radicalization of Dorothy

Chapter 9
Geology – or McCarthyism?

In June, 1933, in the midst of the most disastrous depression in our nation's history, I received my Bachelor of Arts degree from Hunter College. I joined the mass of would-be teachers, lawyers, doctors, engineers, social workers and other professionals who landed in a world in which there were no jobs in our fields and in which everyone scrambled to get whatever work he or she could.

Because I had been an excellent student—both Phi Beta Kappa and *magna cum laude*—the guidance director at Hunter got me a temporary job helping a geology professor who needed routine assistance. I had been a social science major and my knowledge of geology was limited to a vague idea of its definition, but I soon learned how to arrange laboratory samples and the names of the more common specimens that I set up for the students.

I read prodigiously. Sometimes, when I had free time at work, I would return to whatever book I was reading and even, on occasion, discuss it with the geology professor. John Strachey's *The Coming Struggle for Power*, which was in line with the prevailing radical politics of the time and was very well written, seemed a good book to talk about with her—a mild woman without any apparent political convictions.

In those days, the city colleges, of which Hunter was one, were hotbeds of intellectual fervor and left-wing agitation, but I deliberately stayed away from the many campus political organizations. The excuse I gave to myself and to those who urged me to join was that I did not know enough, and I would not "get active" until I was fully conversant with all the facts. I had determined to use my stay in college as a learning experience. This may have only been part of the reason for my aloofness; I *did* want to learn more, but I also think I resented the fact that all through my life to that point, I had been part of a household in which my father fought the garment employers and my mother fought the landlord, and in which we were constantly worried

THE RADICALIZATION OF DOROTHY

about making our seasonal income last for the entire year. My parents' evenings were spent at meetings. Our discussions at home were always vigorous and sometimes bitter and they all dealt with economic and political problems.

I TOOK THE EXAMINATION for a license to teach history in high school. Although there were no openings for teachers, I could, if I passed, be put on a list for future placement. On my application, I listed my geology professor as one of my references. I successfully passed both the written and oral examinations. Then, mysteriously, I was summoned to appear for an additional interview.

While I was waiting in the anteroom, the secretary surreptitiously informed me that the geology professor, when asked for a reference, had characterized me as a "dangerous radical." I was to be interviewed by the State Board of Examiners, whose staff had already investigated my home environment, who knew that left-wing newspapers and other publications were read in the household, and who were preparing to interrogate me about my affiliations. I will always remember with a warm feeling that anonymous secretary who alerted me as to what to expect and gave me the courage to be truthful.

A group of eight men and women, sitting at an oblong table, eyed me suspiciously before bombarding me with questions. I had no difficulty answering them honestly. No, I did not belong to any political organization. Yes, I read Strachey's *The Coming Struggle for Power* and other radical political works. No, I was not then, nor had I ever been....

I expressed my strong objection to the practice of "guilt by association."

I was called back once more for additional grilling, and I repeated my answers. It was evident that the Board had no persuasive evidence to bolster the professor's allegations. My name was subsequently placed on the teachers' list, but I never accepted an appointment.

Ironically, this experience convinced me that I *did* know enough to warrant my becoming active. I had been the victim of an unsubstantiated accusation and had appeared before a bigoted group—which seemed to foreshadow the witch-hunting investigating committees to come—all because of one person's careless conclusion. What I had gone through helped to crystallize my thinking and radicalized me in a way that no amount of theoretical study could have done.

Just prior to these interrogations, I, along with many other professionals, obtained a job as a social investigator in the fast-growing Emergency Relief Bureau (ERB). There, I joined a fledgling union, became an enthusiastic supporter, participating actively, as an unpaid organizer, in its campaigns for job security, higher wages, better working conditions and equal opportunity in the workplace for African-Americans (then called Negroes). The union to which I belonged later became part of the American Federation of State, County and Municipal Employees (AFSCME), which is still, at this writing, the largest national union of public employees in the country.

Chapter 10
The Relief Office and the Union

THE EARLY 1930S WAS A TIME of stark, unadorned contradictions—of dire poverty alongside obscene, ostentatious wealth; of ferment and exhilaration; of deep depression, countered by idealism and buoyant hope; of the unlikely combination of corruption and compassion, as exemplified by New York City's Tammany Hall; and of Italian-suited men, balanced by ragged men in tatters, selling apples on the streets of New York; of club-swinging police attacking and bloodying strikers and unemployed demonstrators. Later on, it became a time when the newly formed Congress of Industrial Organizations (CIO) organized the workers in the automobile, steel, rubber, transport, maritime and electrical industries. And even while racial intolerance was still rife, black and white working men and women were meeting in the same union halls in Detroit, Pittsburgh, and even as far south as Bessemer, Alabama. Formerly rich men, turned penniless by the collapsing stock market, jumped to their deaths from the roofs of their beautiful homes or from their taller office buildings.

With President Franklin D. Roosevelt's New Deal came a proliferation of alphabet agencies, newly constructed public buildings with powerful murals painted by unemployed artists, and thousands of roads, built by workers under the Works Progress Administration (WPA). And, to round out the parade of contradictions, in the White House, guiding these enormous changes, sat a man who was, depending upon whom you asked, either revered or hated, visionary or scorned—the courageous and humane president, who told us that we had "nothing to fear but fear itself," who brought jobs and insurance coverage for the unemployed, food for the hungry, and Social Security for the aged—but, alas! and shamefully, no real help for refugee Jews nor, later, for those in the Nazi concentration camps.

When I graduated from Hunter College in June, 1933, 13 million people—as much as one-quarter of the nation—were unemployed. In New York City, between 1929 and 1932, four hundred social agencies closed their doors.

In 1933, the city's jobless rolls reached two million. There was only one place in town where young people with degrees, fresh out of college, could obtain steady work, and that was at the recently established Emergency Relief Bureau (ERB). Utilizing funds supplied by the federal, state and local governments, the ERB hired 10,000 social investigators and clerical workers to administer the dispensing of "relief." Fiorello H. LaGuardia, the frenetic, vigorous, reform-minded mayor, who was determined to eliminate the Tammany patronage that had permeated the city's governing agencies, emphasized the possession of a college degree as one of the requirements for hiring. Huge numbers of newly minted teachers, social workers, lawyers, scientists, and even some doctors, flocked to the ERB for a steady job paying $27.50 a week for working five and one-half days (half a day on Saturday). I was among those hired.

Precinct offices were set up, first in police stations and later in condemned schools and other abandoned city buildings. My first job location was a former fire station at 188th Street and Webster Avenue in the Bronx. There were constant shortages of envelopes, paper clips and other office supplies, as well as desks and chairs. We dictated the accounts of our investigatory visits into dictaphones, from which they were transcribed into permanent records by pools of typists. Although the rules called for caseloads of 60, we often each dealt with 150 cases, and the number rarely went down to 100. Our basic assignment was to visit families who had qualified for relief during a preliminary interview in our intake office. We were to verify their eligibility and then to continue monthly personal visits to substantiate their ongoing right to home relief.

It was a heartbreaking task. We encountered so much abject poverty, so much hunger, so much frustration, depression and anger! By the summer of 1934, one person in seven in New York City was on home relief. The weekly allowance was pitifully small, hardly enough to pay for basic needs. We were supposed to report if the family had received additional funds through odd jobs, gifts from relatives, or from other sources. What was considered the only positive development was when a family member secured employment and called to close the case. But that rarely happened and our clients had to demean themselves by "begging" for welfare funds.

The last day of the month was particularly difficult because, by then, the welfare families had used up all their funds and the wife or mother would be staring at empty cupboards. On one such day, I still had a long list of visits, and I foolishly decided to make them. I was greeted, in the main, by a combination of loud explosions of vexatious disappointment, screaming and tears. The children, seeing their mothers cry, immediately joined in. Some clients produced written budgets to prove that we never gave them enough; others showed me their bare iceboxes. They all wanted to know why we couldn't increase the size of their checks so they could meet their minimum needs.

I felt completely frustrated. I didn't like being yelled at, especially when there was literally nothing I could do about it. As a result, I did not finish my rounds on Bathgate Avenue, where there were so many steps to climb and where the halls smelled of human waste and unwashed bodies.

When I arrived home, I wasn't hungry, but I was tired, so I went to bed early—and I dreamed. I dreamed that through either a major bookkeeping error or a change of policy, the following month's checks were all raised to meet the clients' fundamental needs. In the dream, when I visited my clients the next day, they were all smiles and optimism. When I awoke in the morning, I, too, was smiling and experiencing a great sense of relief. It did not take long for me to realize that it was only a dream—a dream we all shared that some day, everyone would work and earn enough to meet their family's needs. That brief period of respite from anxiety was so vivid that I still remember it. At that time, the memory of it served to cheer me up whenever I felt low. It also strengthened my belief that some day, we could change the world.

WHEN I CAME TO WORK at the ERB, I discovered a fledgling union—the Association of Workers in Public Relief Agencies (AWPRA), with officers and a number of committees. Along with many others, I strove to build the union so that we could improve our conditions of work. We needed higher pay, shorter hours, smaller caseloads and larger quarters. Through the union, we also cooperated with the organizations of the unemployed that were working to correct some of the most egregious abuses and to create more humane conditions. I became an active member of my local grievance committee, later the president of Precinct Chapter 46 and, still later, assistant director of the citywide membership committee. Women, who made up almost half of the work force and performed much of the union work, occupied important positions in many union chapters, but the top union jobs were always held by men. It was not until World War II, with the departure of men to the armed forces, that many of the most significant positions were allotted to women.

Through our energetic efforts to eliminate work problems, we were able to build a constantly growing, vigorous union, which, by 1935, boasted five thousand members. Through picketing, demonstrating and a good deal of negotiation, we were able to win the first contract ever in a public relief agency. Among the gains we won were the establishment of a joint labor-management panel to hear appeals against disciplinary actions and the setting up of a formal grievance machinery. We celebrated this victory with a Saturday night party to which we invited non-members as well. The contract and the resulting improved status of the union helped convince many of the former reluctant nay-sayers to join our ranks.

At Saturday night gatherings, at spring picnics, at lunch meetings at a wonderful pizza restaurant on Arthur Avenue (an Italian enclave that exists to this day), the staff socialized, talked about work problems, discussed philosophy, had fun and sang songs—the latter on every possible occasion. It was an exciting period, filled with fervor, hope and limitless dreams. Our co-workers were mostly the sons and daughters of first or second generation immigrants and were observant, intelligent and interested—qualities that helped make the rigors of the job less burdensome.

The period was fruitful in other ways as well, resulting in a number of marriages, including my own. After meeting on the picket line several times and then dating, Leonard Jacobson, who was an active member in another precinct, and I were married in 1937, taking a long weekend for our honeymoon. Two years later, for a real honeymoon, we went on a three-week trip to Mexico with another couple, cousins of Leonard. We took a lot of pictures and had a marvelous time. I remember passing, on the way, the cotton fields of Georgia where children seven or eight years old were working. We waved our hands in greeting as we drove past.

We women had many role models, like the tiny, passionate Rose Schneiderman of the Women's Trade Union League (WTUL), whom my mother always considered a person to emulate. There was also Eleanor Roosevelt, whom I first met at a WTUL meeting and who inspired me with her warmth and empathy. I had occasion to speak with her again after she lectured on labor rights at a session I attended at the New York City Central Labor Council.

Our union leaders, led by our president, Abram Flaxer, were fiery, eloquent, tenacious and infectious in their zeal. These qualities helped spark our meetings, as they taught us how to effect change in our work. I had been going downtown regularly, at least three times a week, to our union headquarters, located on Beekman Street in lower Manhattan. I would take the subway downtown, directly after work, stopping at the large deli restaurant (then called a cafeteria) near the union office, gulping down a sandwich and a glass of milk and rushing to a meeting. I finally developed such an aversion to sandwiches that for years thereafter, I would have my main meal for lunch and salads or soups in the evening, just so I would not have to order or even look at a sandwich.

AT THE UNION OFFICE, I attended a membership planning session, an executive board meeting or a special conference with Jack Bigel, who headed the membership committee and was my direct boss and mentor. I tried to absorb as many of our immediate problems as I could, while keeping sight of what was called "the bigger picture." There I met all of the AWPRA leaders, including the dynamic and incredibly knowledgeable president of our Welfare Local 1, Sam Sorkin—along with Henry Wenning, Ewart Guinier, Alan MacKensie and Dan Allen—all top officers in their locals—and Board secretary Dorothy Funt.

Most of them went on to distinguished careers. Ewart was the father of Lani Guinier, who almost became a cabinet member in Bill Clinton's administration. Ewart himself went on to a college professorship and helped launch the African-American studies program at Harvard University; Jack Bigel established his own benefit and pension consulting firm and served as adviser to the Municipal Labor Committee, which encompassed most of the city's public employees' unions. Dorothy Funt was the sister of Allan Funt, originator of the *Candid Camera* television show, and she was one of the early staff members at Martin E. Segal's successful insurance and pension consulting firm. Toward the end of my involvement, Frank Herbst joined the Welfare Department staff, and I helped him develop his organizing skills. He later became president of Local 1 of the United Public Workers of America.

My colleagues at the union headquarters were constantly "kidding" me about my intensity. I would always be asking questions, never content to let anything pass unheeded. I'm sure much of the teasing was caused by the fact that I was a woman, but I didn't let it prevent me from learning a great deal about negotiations, strategy and tactics and organizing skills, as well as the value of perseverance.

This was a period of turmoil and growth in the labor movement. All over the country, in industry after industry, workers were taking advantage of the rights granted by the recently enacted National Labor Relations Act (NLRA), which gave them the right to organize. There were bitter strikes and workers lost their lives on the picket lines. In many states, the National Guard was called out to stifle the workers' right to organize. The period also witnessed the general strike initiated by the West Coast longshoremen in 1934, as well as the sit-down strike at the General Motors plant in Flint, Michigan.

Under the leadership of the newly formed Congress of Industrial Organizations (CIO), unions were organized on an industrial rather than craft basis in such mass production industries as steel, automobile, rubber and maritime. Industrial unionism also brought large numbers of African-Americans, women and immigrant workers into unions for the first time. The newly organized unions were able, one after another, to negotiate contracts guaranteeing job security, higher pay, shorter workdays and improved working conditions. With these gains came expectations of future rewards. We could actually feel the tension, ferment and the sense of hope in the air. We were frequently called upon to help the organizational drives by joining picket lines and sending messages of support to workers on strike.

And the struggles began to bear fruit. As a result of marches, demonstrations and picket lines, in many of which I participated, the developing labor movement was able to persuade President Roosevelt and Congress to enact the Social Security Act. For the first time in our history, our older citizens were guaranteed dignity upon their retirement and were no longer dependent on relatives or government welfare agencies. Disabled workers, no longer able to work, were also able to get financial assistance, as were the families of deceased workers.

The same was true of our successful campaign to win unemployment insurance. This came about after a long struggle within the ranks of the American Federation of Labor. A number of its leaders, including President William Green, joined the employers in branding such legislation as "socialistic." But once again, the unity of the workers, both employed and unemployed, brought about victory and the enactment of national legislation providing this vital benefit.

In September, 1936, the American Federation of State, County and Municipal Employees (AFSCME), under the leadership of Arnold Zander of the Wisconsin State Employees Association, held its first annual convention in Detroit and voted to become part of the AFL. The AWPRA sent 51 delegates to that convention and constituted almost half (40%) of AFSCME's membership. AWPRA Local 1046 Organizer William Gaulden, an African American, was nominated and elected vice-president and was joined on the executive board by AWPRA's president Abram Flaxer and another leader, Russell Stephens. David Kanes of AWPRA's Philadelphia local was elected secretary-treasurer. AWPRA now included locals in such major cities, in addition to New York, as Chicago, Detroit and Philadelphia.

Meanwhile, back in New York City, Mayor Fiorello H. LaGuardia was attempting to live up to his promise to incorporate the Department of Welfare, of which we were now a part, into the civil service structure, so that appointments to positions there would be based on merit, not political patronage. He had already arranged to provide that coverage to the transit and hospital workers without the necessity of their taking examinations. We traveled up to Albany, hundreds strong, to attempt to convince the members of the State Legislature to guarantee permanent status for all our workers.

However, New York City Civil Service Commissioner James Finegan had other ideas. He was determined to make the Department of Welfare employees compete with outside workers for their jobs. He announced that an open, competitive examination would be held that year, 1936, for the jobs we were filling. In Harlem, the dangers posed by Finegan's proposals were crystal clear, and we were able to put together a coalition that included Congressman Adam Clayton Powell, A. Philip Randolph, president of the Brotherhood of Sleeping Car Porters, and the leaders of both the National Negro Congress and of a number of Harlem's largest churches. On February 15, we marched, 15,000 strong, down Broadway toward City Hall. A number of our people were hurt when police, on horseback, charged into our line. I was able, along with a group of other demonstrators, to rush into a local store just in time to escape being knocked down by a policeman's horse that had mounted the sidewalk.

We picketed both Finegan's office and his home. Whenever he announced the test—which he did on four occasions—we doubled the size of our picket lines. Through radio announcements and open-air street corner meetings, we rallied community support for our cause. My cousin, Dr. Gene Falstein, a psychiatrist, who was in town for a convention, happened to walk by while I was addressing a lunch-hour demonstration in the garment center. He waited until I had finished speaking in order to make sure that it was really me.

I don't know which one of us was more surprised, but I do know that he never stopped talking about his ubiquitous, militant cousin.

At a mass meeting held early in November, 1936, 7,000 union members voted to strike. Vito Marcantonio, our spirited, determined lawyer, told Mayor LaGuardia that "we would conduct continuous picketing if we were forced to the wall." Later that month, true to our word, we picketed Finegan's office 24 hours a day, but we were unable to move him, and the examination was set for December 30, on the same terms Finegan had announced.

Early in December, we held a union meeting at which our leaders agreed to conduct a sit-down strike if it became necessary, with the date to be set later. On December 22, just before closing time, at 4:45 p.m., I was called to the telephone in our office and I heard a voice on the other end say, "Now's the time! Assemble your staff!"

Back in the main area of our workplace, at about 5:00 p.m., I jumped up on a table, with the help of several coworkers, called an impromptu emergency meeting to order and asked: "Are we going to give in to Finegan?"

"No!" came the unanimous response.

"Then let's sit down until the city backs down," I shouted. There was loud applause, and we all sat down. We were holding our first sit-down strike! Workers in the other offices, after getting the same message, also sat down. Following the example of the automobile and rubber workers, who had used this tactic so effectively, we sat in overnight.

We sat on the floor, wearing our coats, hats and scarves because it was winter and we knew that at some point, the heat would be turned off. We sang—*We Shall Not Be Moved, Solidarity Forever, Union Maid* and other union songs—which both bolstered our morale and kept us animated and warm. All that night we talked, we ate, and we even slept. We ransacked our briefcases for leftover food and fruit, and our pockets for candy bars. Fortunately, one of the workers had rushed out directly after the vote to buy ham and cheese and packaged bread at a local grocery store. He hurried back in before the night watchman arrived, since he knew that once the watchman was there, no one would be permitted to enter the building.

The next morning, Flaxer called us and told us to return to work. "The Civil Service Commission has still insisted on an exam," he reported, "but they have agreed that 50% of the total mark will be awarded for accumulated service on the job." Because we had remained united and had persevered, we had succeeded in protecting the jobs of our union members! We spent the succeeding years consolidating our gains, increasing the size of our union and working for additional benefits on a national scale.

During the AFL's 1935 convention, the CIO unions, led by the United Mine Workers' president, John L. Lewis, unable to move the AFL to bring unskilled, black and women workers into its ranks, decided to break away and form their own federation. Two years later, our president, Abram Flaxer, impressed by the CIO's efforts to "organize the unorganized" and by its determination to bring the benefits of unionism to hundreds of thousands, and even millions of workers, requested that Zander affiliate the AFSCME union with the CIO. Even though the

CIO had pledged to furnish funds and organizers for a national organizational drive, Zander rejected Flaxer's request. Thereupon, AWPRA's 25,000 members followed Flaxer into the CIO, where they established the State, County and Municipal Workers of America (SCMWA), which, in its heyday, boasted some 300,000 members, and which later became the United Public Workers of America (UPWA).

That same year, 1937, in harmony with the temper of the times, the International Ladies' Garment Workers' Union (ILGWU) sponsored a lively, syncopated musical, *Pins and Needles*, written by Harold Rome. It became an instant hit. During its first week's performances, a group of us went to see it. We loved its energy, its clever lyrics and its fast-moving dances. We left the theater humming *Sing Me a Song with Social Significance*, one of the hit songs of the show—and I have been humming it ever since. The show, incidentally, was so successful that it moved to Broadway, where it enjoyed a long run.

In 1942, I was elected the first woman president of SCMWA's New York State division. I became a symbol of what women could accomplish when men went off to war, or even after they returned. Symbol or not, when I took the oath of office, I was pregnant.

Chapter 11:
The War Years and Beyond: 1941 – 1952

DECEMBER 7, 1941 was a date that had the kind of catastrophic significance for us then that September 11, 2001, has for us now. That was the fateful day of Pearl Harbor, when the Japanese army carried out a sneak attack on the American base in the Pacific, and overnight our lives were changed. The following day, President Roosevelt officially declared war on Japan and two days later, its Axis partners, Germany and Italy, responded by declaring war on us. Our country proceeded to place its resources and its man and womanpower where its sentiments were in that worldwide struggle between freedom and tyranny.

Sudden and duplicitous as the attack on Pearl Harbor was, it came upon a country that had already all but thrown in its lot on the side of the Allies. This was particularly true of the Jewish community here, because the reports of the Nazi onslaught against our blood brothers and sisters, first in Germany itself and later in country after country that fell under the heel of fascism, had an important mobilizing effect on the American Jewish population. And when, earlier that year in June, Hitler sent his troops eastward toward the Soviet Union, and that country and its people began to bear the brunt of the *Wehrmacht* military onslaught, the feelings of the American people toward the Russians underwent a "sea change."

The resentments fueled by the Nazi-Soviet pact in 1939, which precipitated World War II, began to dissolve as word reached us of the heroism and sacrifices of the Russian people. For progressives like myself, already sympathetic toward the Soviet Union, what we had formerly derided as a "phoney war" became, almost overnight, a "just" war, World War II, in which we were fighting alongside our allies in a long, bloody, bitter struggle against Hitler and his Nazi regime.

In response to President Roosevelt's urgent appeals, Leonard and I sold our car in order to save gas. I bought war bonds and saved silver foil, rolling it into balls, just as we had done during World War I. Gas, sugar and meat were on the list of rationed items. I waited on long lines to buy my quota of nylon stockings when they were available. Mama and her co-workers joined the ranks of air raid wardens, checking to see that safety regulations were followed. I have saved a stack of certificates she earned, testifying to her exemplary performance

Then, one day in September, 1943, the telephone in our apartment rang—at least four times—before I could make my son, Bobby, comfortable enough to leave him alone in the crib so I could answer it. He was all of four months old, and I was on a year's maternity leave from the Department of Welfare. When I picked up the phone, a woman's voice informed me that the caller was Hanna Saxon, Executive Director of Russian War Relief (RWR). She went on to say that Gretchen Spiro, a leader of the Furriers' Union, who was about to join the staff of the newly organized Labor-Management Division of Russian War Relief, had recommended me as co-director of the division. Gretchen and I had met at delegates' meetings of the New York City Central Labor Council, where we represented our respective unions, and we had become quite friendly.

I explained to Ms. Saxon that I had not planned to go back to work for some months, but we arranged to meet to discuss the matter further.

By the middle of November, I had hired a nanny and had assumed the position of co-director of Russian War Relief's Labor-Management Division. One of the immediate tasks we faced was bridging the huge ideological gap that separated the U. S. and the USSR. If we could not succeed in that effort, there was no way we would be able to acquire the much-needed food, clothing and medicines for a country that was, at that time, bearing the major brunt of the battle against the Nazi war machine that had swept through much of the European continent. The American people recognized that the armies of the Soviet Union were sustaining millions of casualties and its people suffering considerable hardships. Earlier that year, Leningrad, the country's second largest city, had bravely withstood a 15-month siege. In August of that year, 1943, Winston Churchill had told an American audience, after meeting with Franklin D. Roosevelt and Joseph Stalin: "If we are together, nothing is impossible. If we are divided, all of us will fail."

To further complicate the situation, the American Federation of Labor (AFL) and the Congress of Industrial Organizations (CIO) were still, in 1943, separate organizations with sharply divided organizing philosophies. It was essential that we get the support of both groups if we were to be successful. As a result of careful planning and with the assistance of a number of friends in or close to the labor movement, we were able to obtain the sponsorship of AFL President William Green. This was soon followed by that of CIO President Philip Murray. After that, it was relatively easy to be able to list on our letterhead the names of an additional 60 or so key union leaders from both organizations and from all over the country.

Because the United Way was legally the national fundraiser for organizations like Russian War Relief, we were not permitted to raise funds but were limited to contributions "in kind"—that is, of such items as clothing, medicines and hospital equipment. Harry Uviller, the arbitrator in the ladies' garment industry, chaired the clothing division and William Jay Scheffelin, a leading pharmaceutical manufacturer, chaired the division which collected medicines and hospital equipment. These two gentlemen, effective organizers with extensive knowledge of their respective jurisdictions, performed their tasks with great distinction.

Our organization was able to achieve remarkable results by working with industry leaders, by involving the union leaderships and their rank-and-file members and by taking full advantage of the combination of patriotic fervor and anti-Nazi sentiment that was at its height in our country during that period. We sponsored rallies with outstanding entertainers, sent out scores of mailings and reached out to people through personal phone calls. As a result, we were able to acquire huge amounts of scarce, badly needed items and to forward them to the Eastern European Front. As part of our campaign, we arranged a celebration that was attended by a Red Army commander who was visiting this country for which the Bakers' Union prepared a towering, 17-layer cake, bedecked with handsome U.S. and Soviet flags.

When the Russians and Americans became fighting allies during World War II, the lessening of antagonisms between them helped to dispel some of the hostility that was expressed toward this country's immigrants. This was especially true when some of the world's most prestigious cultural and intellectual figures who were refugees from Nazi Germany—such as Albert Einstein, Thomas Mann, Bertolt Brecht, Kurt Weill and Lotte Lenya—were welcomed into this country.

It was also the period when Jews all over the United States frantically sought help in bringing their relatives here out of the grasp of the deadly Hitler-inspired anti-Semitism that was all too prevalent in Eastern Europe. This was true of my family as well. Mama and her sisters had raised sufficient funds and guarantees to bring their mother, Grandma Anna, into this country. She was in her eighties, frail, yet dignified, and still evidencing the loveliness in her face that reflected itself in her daughters' beauty. When my son, Bobby, was three years old, she stayed with us for several months. He was the first great-grandchild she was able to enjoy in this country.

However, it was difficult for her to adjust to this very strange world—to the tall buildings, the many languages and the strains of urban living. When she moved to Chicago to live with my mother's sister, Aunt Anna, she still had a great deal of difficulty coping with the bewildering differences that were part of life there as well.

Previously, Mama and her sisters had confronted the urgent need to bring their sister, Mary, and her children here from the Soviet Union, where they lived under the constant threat posed by the invading Nazi army. Mama desperately searched for the sponsorship that was necessary to accomplish this. Through careful research, she learned that Eugene Picker, an official of the Loew's movie theatre chain, was related to us on Papa's side of the family. She somehow managed to set up an appointment to visit him at his office. She told us how impressed she was by the lavish office furnishings and the evident magnitude of his business activities. More important, however, was the kindness he displayed toward her and his willingness to be of assistance. Apparently, she had convinced him to accept the responsibility of sponsoring Aunt Mary and her family. She met with him several times in preparation.

Unfortunately, however, when she returned, as planned, several months later to consummate the arrangements, she was stunned to learn that he had died and left no written evidence of his commitment. No one in his office could confirm the entire episode. Such disappointment! Such anguish! Mama was distraught for months; even more so when we learned that Mary and most of her family had been destroyed by the Nazis.

We made no further effort to contact the Picker family. However, their name did appear in print recently in Aaron Lansky's book, *Outwitting History*. I was pleased to note his reference to Arnold Picker, Eugene's younger brother, who had a distinguished career as a movie producer at United Artists before he died in 1989. Lansky calls him a friend and helper in his own campaign to retrieve Jewish books, a campaign in which he has been so spectacularly successful.

In 1944, during President Roosevelt's campaign for reelection to a fourth term, I received permission, in response to a request from the election committee, to take the summer off to assist in the operation. I established a "Doctors for Roosevelt" division on whose letterhead were listed, among others, a number of famous psychiatrists of the period. The group not only raised funds, but also did effective organizational work as well. This was particularly important because the dominant organization of medical practitioners, the American Medical Association (AMA), was strongly opposed to many of Roosevelt's initiatives and fought vigorously against him.

In April, 1945, President Roosevelt died, and a month later the war in Europe ended. Within a short time, the political atmosphere of the country underwent a substantial change. It was symbolized by Winston Churchill's "Iron Curtain" speech in Fulton, Missouri in 1946, which represented a 180-degree turn from the position he had enunciated three years earlier.

THE COLD WAR SET IN. In 1947, the Taft-Hartley law was enacted over President Harry Truman's veto and the labor movement, around which so much of my life had revolved, entered a period of turmoil and division that was seized upon by the employers. One of the objectionable features of the Taft-Hartley law was a requirement that the leaders of unions desiring to utilize the facilities of the National Labor Relations Act—such as in representation elections—sign what were called "non-Communist affidavits." This was followed, shortly thereafter, by a decision at a CIO convention to expel 11 unions for being under Communist leadership. One of the unions expelled was the United Public Workers of America, whose president at the time was Abram Flaxer, with whom I had worked during my union organizing days in New York City's Department of Welfare. As a result of the expulsions, a number of unions, instead of concentrating their efforts on the repeal of the Taft-Hartley law, took advantage of its "non-Communist affidavit" feature to conduct raids against unions that were not in compliance. Thus, instead of carrying out labor's natural function of organizing the unorganized, these unions devoted their energies to "unorganizing the organized."

Other provisions of this aptly named "Slave Labor" law included the banning of secondary boycotts, through which unions could support each other in strikes (there had been seven general strikes in the U. S. in 1946 and the employers were determined to drive a spike into such expressions of solidarity), and a provision that made possible the passage by states of the so-called "right-to-work" laws, which forbade the signing of union-shop agreements. Today, almost 60 years after its passage, the Taft-Hartley law is still wreaking havoc on the labor movement.

THE WAR YEARS AND BEYOND

Meanwhile, at home, our family was gradually dispersing. Ethel left home when she married in 1932. I left in 1937. Papa died in January, 1940. That same year, Irving was drafted into the army and three years later, Donald applied to become an Air Corps pilot.

Mama was now alone in our latest dwelling on Simpson Street, still in the Bronx. Instead of seeking boarders, as she had in the past, she decided to move in with a friend and activist colleague, Celia Vosk, who had just lost her husband and was in need of both company and financial help. The results were disastrous; the two women fought constantly over even the most minor issues and Mama sought desperately for a solution.

There were major changes in my home as well. Our nanny, a second generation German immigrant, turned out to be a most unfortunate choice. Although an excellent cook, preparing mouth-watering roast pork, *sauerbraten* and other delicacies, her cooking strained the limit of her creative abilities. When I came home early in the day, I usually found her sitting, stone-faced and stolid, next to Bobby's carriage. She performed her tasks in silence and without a smile, whether it was feeding Bobby, diapering him or rocking him in his carriage when he cried; she never showed any emotion and she never played with him or read to him. Rigid and taciturn, she might just as well have been a robot. Bobby needed warmth and affection, and I was compelled to let her go.

At the same time, my marriage was coming to a close. The euphoric excitement generated by our building a union together faded when Leonard changed careers in 1940, and became a theatrical agent. Although we shared political convictions, our everyday experiences were now vastly different. Neither of us seemed willing to adjust to the other's interests and soon after Bobby was born, we separated by mutual consent. We made the necessary arrangements for child visitation. Leonard's sisters tried valiantly to bring us together again, but I held firm. This may seem somewhat cold and calculated, but it was the culmination of a swirling stream of thoughts that had disturbed

A SONG OF SOCIAL SIGNIFICANCE   89

me for months and that had resulted in many sleepless nights. After all, how could I, who preached perseverance to others, give up what was intended to be a lifelong relationship? Was I, who had played a helpful role in so many other people's lives, a failure in my own?

I realized that our relationship had been formed in a period when love and mating were in the air and when we were both part of an exciting movement. I also realized that, at the age of 24, I had felt it was time for a permanent relationship. Not even Ethel, my fun-loving sister, had waited beyond that age to get married.

It was then that I realized that what I missed in Leonard was the quality of tenacity. Even though he was handsome, bright and cultured, I felt that he did not work hard enough for the things he desired, either in the union, or in his new capacity as a theatrical agent. It was that quality that I found indispensable and since I could not change him, I could only change the situation we were in.

As a result, Mama came to live with Bobby and me. They loved each other very much and, for many years, Mama was an important part of his life.

We were living at the time at 1195 Anderson Avenue in the West Bronx, in a complex of six similar apartment buildings built in the mid-1920s and located on a steep hill. We lived on the fourth floor, but at least there was an elevator. When the buildings were constructed, they were quite elegant and even boasted a doorman and oriental rugs and a comfortable settee in the spacious lobby. By the time we moved in, all three were long gone. What there was, however, was reasonable rent and the usual one month's concession. We remained there until 1962, when I moved to downtown Manhattan.

Unlike the house in which I was born, nearly all the tenants were Jewish. Also, unlike my earlier home, the Jewish boys were constantly having run-ins with the Irish kids who lived one block farther west on Woodycrest Avenue and who attended parochial school. The Irish boys would shout "Christ-killer" and "kike" at Jewish kids traveling alone or in small groups on Woodycrest Avenue or throw cinders at them and beat them up. We sent delegations to meet with the priest at the local church to which the school was attached. It took a number of heated discussions to persuade him to deal effectively with the problem. The fights tapered off, but they did not stop completely.

There were many building complaints—insufficient heat and hot water, leaks, etc.—and to deal with them, we set up a committee which I was chosen to chair. My second-in-command was a policeman. We met with the landlord and were fortunately able to resolve many of our issues without having to take drastic action.

Just as my mother had before me, I became friendly with a number of neighbors after I had settled in our apartment. My closest friend was Lil Waldman, a gregarious Renaissance woman who lived on the fifth floor with her husband and son. She was skilled in just about every area of the creative arts and she knew everybody. She was a gourmet cook, a consummate baker, a painter, a ceramist, a clothing designer, a seamstress, an art historian, a connoisseur of fine objects, a fabricator of jewelry—and a good friend. I learned a great deal from her, and she lent me many children's books, including the Dr. Seuss series. Her son, Marty, was three years older than Bob, who continued advancing to Marty's reading level. While growing up, the two boys had different interests, but today they have a great deal in common and have become good friends.

Lil and I went to museums, attended concerts, and enjoyed many delicious meals together, the best of which were those Lil cooked herself. We remained close friends until she died a few years ago.

WHILE WORKING at Russian War Relief, I met many of the younger labor leaders, including Leon Davis, the first president of Local 1199. His wife, Julia, had been one of my co-workers at the Emergency Relief Bureau. He and his members played a major role in helping us collect medicines. At a fund-raising event for our drive, at which the musicians performed without charge, I met William Feinberg, the much admired president of Musicians' Union, Local 802. When he invited me to a reception at the famous Stork Club, I was able to observe the deference shown him by the club's legendary owner, Sherman Billingsley. And because I was with Feinberg, I received a bottle of the Stork Club's special perfume, along with a gallant, European-style hand kiss from Billingsley.

Michael Quill, the feisty leader of the Transport Workers Union, always impressed me with his astuteness, his humor —and his brogue, which seemed to become thicker each time I heard him speak. I also received much useful advice, as well as access to a considerable amount of material, from Michael De-Cicco, the president of the Furniture Workers' Union. And Ben Gold, the fiery, beloved president of the Fur Workers' Union, had his members fashion fur-lined vests for the Russian soldiers. Theirs was one of the most useful contributions, and I called Gold to tell him how much it was appreciated. So it did not quite come as a surprise when Gold offered me the job of administrator of a brand new project—a dental clinic for members of his union where they could receive superior dental care at reasonable prices.

Gold had conceived of this idea while talking with his own dentist, Dr. Abe Weinstein, the renowned "dentist to the stars." Among his patients were Hollywood luminaries, corporate executives and prominent professionals. His specialty was "reconstruction of the mouth" and he was noted for both the attractiveness and endurance of his work. It was Gold's dream that workers, too, could share the benefits of Weinstein's unique skills. He believed that if the profit element was eliminated, it would be possible to charge reasonable fees.

The union constructed a small dental clinic on the premises of the Furriers Joint Council at 250 West 26th Street. There were offices for six dentists, a laboratory and a waiting room. Frank Bisk was the dentist in charge, and the other dentists were Abe Geissner, Ferris Henry, a West Indian woman and the wife of union leader Lyndon Henry, Bernard Scheitin and Bernard Bender. All had been carefully interviewed to assure the union of their competence. They worked part-time at an agreed-upon wage. Dr. Weinstein, who worked *pro bono*, would come in regularly to assure that standards were adhered to and also for consultation about difficult problems.

My job was to see that the clinic ran smoothly, to supervise the staff, and, with some clerical help, to arrange scheduled appointments. I would consult with each patient about the type of work needed and discuss the appropriate fees, all carefully determined in advance and provided on printed lists. I was very much aware that I was part of a pioneering effort that had few, if any, predecessors. The members of the Joint Council, in whose building the clinic was located, had firsthand knowledge of the clinic and made good use of its facilities. Henry Foner, then the educational director of the Fur Dressers and Dyers Joint Board, another section of the union, helped to publicize the clinic among the members of his union.

On paper, it looked like a wonderful idea. It soon turned out, however, that the cost of maintaining such an operation was considerably greater than the income provided by the affordable fees and the union was not able to make up the difference from its treasury. Since none of the principals, including the union, were willing to compromise on the quality of the services, it was decided to terminate the project after about a year. It took a number of years thereafter before unions were able to include dental care in their negotiated health benefits.

Some of the administrative procedures we used were so innovative that we were visited by representatives of several group dental services. I was invited to consult with the officers of a large nonprofit dental group in Washington. I spent a week analyzing their methods and then prepared a written set of recommendations. I still have the letter of appreciation for my services.

DURING THE WAR YEARS, I RECEIVED MANY LETTERS from my brothers and from friends and acquaintances. Those that were sent from overseas came in what were called "v-mails," which were condensed in size in order to facilitate mailing. One that I received from someone I had known while growing up in the Bronx—1st Lieutenant Samuel Plotnick—read:

May 1, 1945
Detachment HQ
245th Quartermaster Battalion
Somewhere in Belgium

Dear Dorothy:

It seems that every or almost every national group in the world, except our own, has little or no prejudice against the Negro. From articles I've read by Roi Ottley, the English treat him as an individual. In Paris, I have seen the Negro accepted by his white neighbors both socially and intellectually. There, even intermarriage is not looked down upon so as to almost forbid it. Here in Belgium, I see the Negro soldiers participating in social activities with the populace. The same courtesies are extended to him as his white confrère enjoys at the hands of the very friendly inhabitants here.

The same is true in one of our colonies, Puerto Rico. I'm assigned to an all-Puerto Rican outfit and I have observed the relations between Negroes and whites. I find they are most cordial.

Our own country seems to stand out alone as still practicing the racial prejudice we have fought in peace, and now in war. This attitude is reflected in the lives of our own soldiers, where I'm told that every so often, armed white soldiers descend upon

Negro groups who are located nearby, and the
Negroes return to their commanding officers (white),
demanding or pleading to know why it must be so.

I SPENT THE NEXT FEW YEARS RAISING FUNDS for progressive,
nonprofit organizations, including the American Jewish Labor
Council, which had been established by a number of progressive
unions to combat both anti-Semitism and racism. An effective
fund-raising tool of the Council was its annual three-day holiday bazaar, held at the St. Nicholas Arena, a large hall located
near the site of the present Lincoln Center and used for prize
fights.

The sponsors of the bazaar would obtain contributions of new
clothing, art objects, appliances, jewelry, books, toys, glassware,
leather goods and other desirable merchandise. Supporters of
the bazaar included manufacturers, unions, rank-and-file groups,
such as the garment workers and the hat, cap and millinery
workers, large numbers of individuals, and retail store owners,
who rented booth space. (One of the latter was so successful
that he later opened a chain of stores in various parts of the city.)
For months in advance, the millinery workers fashioned beautiful hats, the hatters turned out their fedoras and caps (almost
everyone wore headwear in those days) and the cloakmakers
and dressmakers, skirts and dresses. Groups of women sewed
exquisite children's outfits and knitted baby sweaters, blankets,
scarves and gloves. There was also a full-service restaurant on
the premises.

The American Jewish Labor Council, for which I worked, had
had just one bazaar before I came on board. It had been planned
and carried out by Bill Levner, the organization's executive director. It had been highly successful, so I decided to try it again.
Bill made available both his files and his very sage advice. Since
we were working with all volunteer help, the job was enormous,
but the energy that was generated and the creative ability that
was demonstrated, as well as the dedication shown, were truly
inspiring. We received free publicity in a number of papers,

including the Jewish *Morning Freiheit* and the progressive afternoon newspaper, *PM*. We always finished the bazaar with a festive occasion at which everyone was appropriately thanked. In the post-World War II period, when progressive organizations were under constant attack, the fund-raising provided by these bazaars played an increasingly crucial role in keeping the organizations afloat.

It was around this time that I received a phone call from Congressman Vito Marcantonio asking me to come to his office. I remembered him as "Marc," our union attorney who had fought so resolutely and successfully for us during our civil service campaigns. I knew him also as the representative of the 20th Congressional District in East Harlem, who, during his 14years in Congress, had been a consistent and courageous fighter for the people in his district and for civil rights and economic justice. I had campaigned for him several times, going from door to door and being cordially invited in to make my presentation. I don't know of any public figure who was so beloved by his constituents, and he was certainly the only congressman whose office was open every day of the year, with Marc, himself, being present every Saturday, Sunday and Monday. If he could not converse with the person seeking help, he had translators in Italian, Spanish, Hungarian, Polish and Yiddish.

I will never forget the Sunday afternoon I came to his headquarters to go canvassing and saw a long line of men, women and children that snaked around the block leading to his main office on First Avenue at 77th Street. Curious, I looked inside. There was Marc, sitting on a platform, with three secretaries taking notes and, waiting in their assigned places, experts on welfare, jobs, health care, housing, immigration and personal problems. I learned later that he saw and spoke to about 30,000 constituents a year. Case by case, he was able to stave off countless evictions and deportations and to secure welfare and other payments for hundreds of his constituents.

While it was very unusual, we never considered it strange that he regularly won all three party primaries in his district—

Democratic, Republican and American Labor Party (ALP)—
although he chose to be listed only under the ALP. The latter
had been established before Roosevelt's reelection campaign in
1936 by a number of unions whose leaders were seeking a way to
support FDR without having to be associated with Tammany
Hall, the controlling force of New York's Democratic Party.
Among the ALP's leaders at the time of its birth were ILGWU
President David Dubinsky and the president of the Amalgamated
Clothing Workers of America, Sidney Hillman. The ALP was
credited with playing a major role in garnering labor support for
Roosevelt. However, by the late 1940s, Dubinsky had departed
from the ALP over the issue of "Communist influence." and,
together with Alex Rose, the president of the Hat, Cap and
Millinery Workers Union, had been instrumental in forming
the Liberal Party.

As for Marc, even when his district was gerrymandered and
increased in size in an effort to unseat him, he was able to con-
found his enemies and win. It was only when three parties, the
Democrats, the Republicans and the Liberal Party, got together
and ran one candidate against him that he was defeated.

During Marc's tenure in Congress, only one other congressman, Leo Isaacson in the Bronx, was elected on the ALP line
alone. Leo, who had known me when I headed the union in the
welfare office in which his wife worked, offered me a position as
his chief of staff, but I respectfully declined it.

It was against this background that I responded to Marc's
call and came to his office. He was then heading the ALP and
seeking to build it into a strong, independent party. He wanted
me to help him raise funds. I told him that I was seriously
considering moving into private industry so that I could spend
more time with my son. He persuaded me to postpone this for a
year—and then for another.

We organized the holiday bazaars of December, 1951, and
December, 1952, which were both great successes. Marc invited
me to his 50ᵗʰ birthday party on December 10, 1952. We were a
small, intimate group—his wife, Miriam, his campaign man-

ager, Lil Landau, his close adviser and executive secretary of the ALP, Arthur Schutzer, and a few other close friends. We toasted Marc, drank some, told "tall" stories (Marc had a sharp sense of humor) and sang songs. Marc was induced to perform a solo, singing *September Song* from *Knickerbocker Holiday* beautifully. He presented me with a small gold wristwatch engraved *"To Dorothy Epstein, In Appreciation, American Labor Party, 12/52."* (It was decidedly like Marc to share the limelight). For me, it was an unforgettable occasion, made even more poignant by the fact that less than two years later, in August, 1954, Marc dropped dead of a heart attack. He had been planning to run for Congress again, as an independent. On his desk was the first set of nominating petitions with which he had hoped to launch his campaign.

IN JULY, 1950, AN AD IN THE NEWSPAPER, *PM*, read: "Lovely farmhouse near Danbury, Connecticut, pleasant rooms, country atmosphere, wholesome, home-cooked meals, swimming nearby, excellent entertainment."

I had been working very hard at the American Jewish Labor Council and was due a vacation. This ad, promising greenery, good food and entertainment, seemed to provide the place in which I could relax. Bobby was going with Mama to stay at a friend's cottage in the colony at Golden's Bridge in Putnam County, New York.

I arranged by phone to share a room (there were no singles available) and to go up by train the following Sunday, when their week began. I would be picked up at the station in time for lunch. I arrived at our destination and saw a large crowd on the front lawn, near the farmhouse. They seemed to be having a great time, laughing uproariously. I joined the group that was exchanging witticisms—crack, crack, crack, crack—as fast and as sharp as ping pong shots. One woman was particularly hilarious, and when she spoke, the laughter exploded every few minutes. Then the bell for lunch rang. I found myself seated next to Annie Dee, the funny one. She had arrived just an hour before I did. She had heard that the food was good, but the portions small. She smiled and said, "I eat very little. This is your chance to team up with someone whose plate you can pick." I couldn't tell if she was joking, but I was glad to have met such an interesting person even before I had unpacked.

Annie and I really hit it off. She hadn't been kidding about the food. She left half of her main dish on her plate, which Jerry (another new arrival who sat on the other side of her) and I quickly gobbled up. She was a war divorcee whose husband had found another woman. She was an organizer for the United Electrical, Radio and Machine Workers (UE) which was seeking to organize a group of small defense plants in western Pennsylvania. She lived with a friend in Greenwich Village in New York and traveled home most weekends. She had just bought a small British car (this was the era of small cars that saved on fuel) and her trip to the Connecticut farm was the first extended ride she took in it. We spent the time together touring the countryside, enjoying the scenery and giving Annie more experience driving her new car. When we were both scheduled to leave on the following Sunday, we learned that our tablemate, Jerry, was also going home. She somehow squeezed Jerry Maguire, six feet, two inches—a longshoreman built like a football lineman, with ankles as thick as my thighs—into the tiny space available. Somehow, we made it safely back to New York, laughing all the way. (Later, we laughed again, this time with relief, at our recklessness in taking this trip with a new driver).

While we were at the farmhouse, Annie was always a big hit at the informal gatherings just before mealtime. The guests assembled at least a half hour in advance. It was a combination of enjoying the spontaneous repartee and being very hungry. They wanted to be near the door when the bell rang. On the day before we left, the management offered Annie a week's free room and board if she would stay on as an entertainer, but her job prevented her from accepting.

There were a number of talented entertainers who apprenticed there for room and board. In fact, that week, Harry Belafonte "sang for his supper." It was an excellent way in which young talent could be recognized. In the Catskill Mountains in upstate New York, such stars as Danny Kaye, Sid Caesar and Jackie Mason, among many others, made their debuts at the resort hotels that once existed in such large numbers in that area.

For the next eight years, Bob, Annie and I spent our Sundays having picnics at Palisades Park, going to the amusement parks at Rye Beach and Coney Island, and to all kinds of state fairs to enjoy the food and gape at the prize-winning animals. We took an eight-day trip to Quebec, where Bobby picked up some French; we drove up the Bronx and Saw Mill River Parkways to explore some of the scenic routes in upstate New York. Sometimes, Mama joined us, but she was usually busy with her own organization, the recently formed Emma Lazarus Federation. When Bob went to Boy Scout camp near Port Jervis, New York, Annie drove me up to visit him. All in all, this was a glorious period. I called it "Sunny Sunday Time" in which we light-heartedly shared new adventures in new places. For Annie and me, who both worked hard, these trips served many purposes, a chance to be with Bobby, to have fun together, and to discuss both our work and the state of the world. After Annie left her organizing job at the UE, she went on to work in the civil rights movement.

As Bob began to develop his own interests and activities with his own friends, the weekly trips became less frequent, but Annie and I continued them intermittently, visiting the Tanglewood concerts in the Berkshires, near Lenox, Massachusetts, where we enjoyed nature's change of seasons. In 1966, Annie and I took our first trip to Europe.

When she moved to Florida after she retired in 1982, I missed her very much. On business trips to Florida, I made sure to visit her in her co-op apartment in West Palm Beach, where she volunteered to serve as an ombudsman between the members of the co-op and the Board of Directors. Eventually, she entered a nursing home, since she suffered from macular degeneration and had become blind. We talked every week, and Bobby also called her to reminisce. There was certainly plenty to reminisce about.

Annie died in June, 2004, just a month before her 87th birthday. She left her small nest egg to the West Palm Beach Library, where she had been active. The funds will be used to build a small reading park, which will be named in her honor.

MAMA CONTINUED TO MOVE from one community organization to another. The names changed, but her activities remained basically the same. In 1951, the Progressive Women's Council, the successor to the United Council of Working Class Housewives, became the Emma Lazarus Federation of Jewish Women's Clubs (ELF), named after the distinguished Jewish poet whose verse graces the Statue of Liberty. The new organization set as its goals the struggle against anti-Semitism, the promotion of Jewish culture and the fight against all forms of discrimination, whether based on race, ethnicity or gender. ELF had a distinguished career of almost forty years during which its members participated in demonstrations, letter-writing campaigns and petition drives—all aimed at achieving a just and peaceful society.

One of Mama's friends in ELF, and, like her, a charter member, was Clara Lemlich Shavelson. She is remembered as the heroine of the 1909 strike of the shirtwaist workers—the teenage girl who rushed to the platform at the meeting at Cooper Union called to discuss a general strike. "I am a working girl," she said passionately in Yiddish, "one of those striking against intolerable conditions. I am tired of listening to speakers who talk in generalities. I offer a resolution that a general strike be declared—now!" The entire assemblage rose to second her resolution. By the time the strike was over, the local's membership had grown from slightly more than 100 members to 10,000. Clara Lemlich became a national figure and 40 years later, still under 60 years of age, she was an indefatigable fighter for civil rights and against injustice.

Mama served as president of her local ELF group and was reelected regularly. Every one of her fifth-year birthdays, starting at 65 and through her 85th, became the occasion for a fundraising luncheon. She never ceased raising funds. My own close friends were not immune to her efforts, and they all admired her determination.

When she reached 80, Mama entered the new Daughters of Jacob assisted-living facility called Findlay House, located in the Bronx. She was glad to have her own apartment and not to have to worry about cooking or shopping. At 85, she was operated on successfully for colon cancer. When I questioned her wonderful doctor about surgery at her advanced age, he told me: "It's urgent and will save and extend her life. I would recommend this treatment for my own mother." He was right, for Mama had a complete recovery.

At 91, Mama went into the hospital again. One week later, on the night before Mother's Day, 1979, she died. Her young woman doctor told me that she had spent time every day at Mama's bedside, listening to episode after episode of her remarkable life.

Part V
The Vitamin Story

Chapter 12
Back to the ABC's

LIKE SO MUCH ELSE IN MY LIFE, the next chapter of my story began quite by chance. The reader will recall that in 1951, I had agreed to conduct two fund-raising bazaars for Vito Marcantonio and the American Labor Party before I moved into private industry. I had done so in the hope that that this would permit me to spend more time with Bob.

While discussing the second bazaar with Marc, we decided that since we had previously been so successful allocating from three to six months for the planning and execution of the project, we could collect more, sell more and make more if we expanded this period to a full year. I now believe that Marc proposed the extension in order to guarantee that I would remain around to supervise the activity.

The task of accumulating goods over a period of a year required the availability of space in a geographic area that was easily accessible, with attention to such important details as adequate loading facilities and proper temperature. A friend mentioned that he knew a sympathetic person with extra room in his stockroom, located on lower Broadway. By following this lead, we were able to secure, free of charge, a large empty area suitable for our purpose.

Since the arrangement fitted our needs perfectly, we worked hard to make sure that we caused as little disruption as possible of our benefactor's business. During my regular trips to the storage facility to appraise the contributions of goods and to plan the logistics for the coming bazaar, I sometimes had an opportunity to chat with our hosts—three partners in a wholesale health foods distribution company called Balanced Foods. They were energetic, intelligent and friendly. The person I spoke with most frequently was the president, Sam Reiser, and from our conversations, I learned a great deal about their operation. He, in turn, expressed an interest in my future plans. Still, it came as a distinct surprise when, after the successful bazaar and during one of my final trips to the storage area, I was offered the position of regional sales manager. The incumbent manager was contemplating leaving to set up his own business. "We feel you're a likely prospect to replace him," Reiser said. Since the health food industry was made up largely of "Mom-and-Pop" operations, the partners felt it would be a wise move to place a woman in this key position. I was grateful for the opportunity to set a precedent in this field.

During my visits to the facility, I had been fascinated by the many strange labels I had seen as I walked through on my way to our storage area. My curiosity was piqued by such titles as brewer's yeast, blackstrap molasses, wheat germ, a variety of exotic honeys, bone meal, safflower oil and various formulations of vitamins, as well as by the shelves filled with books on nutrition. It had struck me that this was a brand new field with great potential for expansion. The general public was becoming much more nutrition-conscious because of the greater use of refined foods and a growing recognition of the dangers posed by chemical food additives, along with polluted air and water and a host of other emerging problems. I realized that here was another area, quite different from the activities I had pursued in the past, in which one could contribute to the betterment of society.

Knowing that I was almost finished with my task of supervising the bazaar, I had previously agreed to take on the job of bookkeeper for one of Marc's supporters who had a large wholesale bakery in the Bronx. This arrangement, designed to cover the interim period before I entered private industry, was strictly conditional, since I was sure that I possessed neither the skill nor the desire for the kind of work required. I must qualify the statement about my desire for the job. It certainly did not apply to the products being merchandised. As a result, by the fall of 1953, after I had found a highly qualified bookkeeper to replace me at the bakery, I was several pounds heavier than when I had started work there, and my first activity upon entering my new job was to go on a diet.

On several occasions before I began working at Balanced Foods, I had stopped by the facility in order to become better acquainted with the products and their, to me, strange no-menclature. It was almost like learning a new language. I went through a number of the books on the shelves and asked a great many questions of my future employers and the man I was set to replace.

I discovered that a new industry had been born in the late 1890s as a result of the use by the flour millers of more sophisticated refining machinery. The milling process, which removed the germ from wheat and other whole grains, produced an attractive but nutritionally inadequate white flour. In the course of the process, large amounts of some 22 vitamins and minerals were destroyed. Dr. Paul Dudley White, the famous heart specialist, attributed the increasing number of heart attacks after 1900 to this refining of our foods. In 1941, the government, convinced of the need for a more nutritious flour to produce the stronger bodies needed for the war effort, approved the addition of four of the elements that had been destroyed in the milling—Niacin, Thiamin, Riboflavin and Iron—and permitted the manufacturers to call their product "enriched."

The first vitamin, B1 (Thiamin) had been discovered by Casimir Funk in 1911. It was he who coined the word "vitamin." This was followed a short time later by the isolation of Vitamin C by a Hungarian physician named Dr. Albert Szent-Gyorgyi, which earned him a Nobel Prize. Dr. Roger Williams, the eminent scientist, discovered Pantothenic Acid (another B vitamin). Soon after I started work at Balanced Foods, a pair of Canadian brothers, Drs. Evan V. and Wilfrid A. Shute, isolated Vitamin E to great acclaim and excitement.

The pioneer retailers of these health foods, as well as many of the manufacturers and distributors, were unique. They were both idealistic and strong believers in good health and in the natural way to achieve it. The monetary rewards were often of secondary importance to them. It was relatively easy to start a retail business in the field, since it only cost about $500.00 to stock a small store. I'm sure that many of these early retailers, including the owners of the "Mom-and-Pop" stores, enjoyed the sensation of being their own bosses and being able to give expression to their own ideas. They had strong convictions, which they expressed passionately and sometimes fanatically. Some came out of the *Reformhaus* movement, which began in Germany during the 19th Century and was deeply immersed in natural foods, herbs and related products. Others had themselves been ill and had found they could help solve their own health problems through a combination of diet, nutrition and exercise. And then, of course, there were the Americans of all ethnic groups—all firm believers in the concept of natural living.

Joining were scientists like Dr. Linus Pauling, the renowned Nobel Prize winner and himself a dedicated supporter of vitamin supplementation, having done much of his research on Vitamin C. To this list should be added the lecturers, writers, magazine publishers, such as J.I. Rodale of *Prevention*, and physical culturists, like Paul Bragg, Bernarr MacFadden and Bob Hoffman, some of whom also published magazines emphasizing the value of health and exercise. Many of these proponents promoted their ideas and products by visiting all the areas in the country that contained health food stores, which, at that time, were few and far between. They appealed to everyone—men and women, young and old, skinny and obese. A number of prominent movie stars, including Greta Garbo, Gloria Swanson, Robert Cummings, Eddie Albert, Van Johnson and Danny Kaye, lent both glamour and prestige to the movement through their endorsements.

During the 1920s, refined foods, saturated fats, sugar-loaded, additive-laden cereals and other depleted foods had been rapidly replacing the healthier, less convenient foods of earlier years. It was in reaction to this development that the new health foods industry began to attract public awareness, reaching its first major breakthrough in the 1930s. Its organizational component was the National Nutritional Foods Association (NNFA), established in 1939 and representing all-natural food-selling entities. One of its rules was that only retailers were permitted to run for president of the organization, which was obviously intended to consolidate that group's control of the new organization.

It was during that same year, 1939, that Balanced Foods was formed by two brothers, Sam and Will Reiser, both with science degrees from Cornell University. They had learned about the field from a cousin, a successful health food magazine publisher. They added as a partner one of the industry's pioneers—a respected and popular writer, Dr. Maurice Shefferman, familiarly known to the industry as "Doc." By the time I joined their staff in 1953, they were well accepted in the New York metropolitan area, their largest customer base. They also had customers in some of the Midwestern states and as far south as Florida. Their main competitor was Sherman Foods, which had been established in New York City during the early 1920s. They also had to face serious competition from a number of local distributors in other areas.

My job was to increase business by both opening new stores and getting the existing customers to expand their purchases. I started out with great enthusiasm, using many of the organizational techniques I had employed in my previous activities. Orders were taken mainly over the phone, in accordance with weekly schedules arranged by geographic location. Balanced Foods had its own truck, which made deliveries in the metropolitan New York area. I quickly learned that the title of regional sales manager was simply a euphemism for the more direct term of "order taker," and I was soon writing all the orders. Before long, I had trained two clerical workers to record these customer orders while I was either on another call or otherwise unavailable. Plunging directly into the work was somewhat like jumping into the water before I knew how to swim, but I was constantly asking questions and learning through hands-on experience. No customer would receive an answer without my checking!

The established schedule required making calls from Monday through Thursday. I used Friday to study the inventory listings, review customers' former orders, become acquainted with the shipping supervisor and operations, and, of course, ask more questions. I also began visiting customers to become familiar with their problems, discover new products that were on their shelves, and offer them advice, which they were quick to accept. I enrolled in a merchandising course at the Baruch Business School branch of City College. And all the while, in addition to encouraging the sale of all health products, I was promoting vitamins, which were becoming increasingly accepted as food supplements.

Sam Reiser did all the buying for the company, while "Doc" Shefferman prepared our advertising bulletins and handled the public relations. I met regularly with both of them. In consultation with Sam, I established bonus plans for our customers. I utilized the products of Dr. Eugene Schiff, a pharmacist and one of the founders of the industry who produced a highly popular line of natural vitamins under the Schiff label, which can still be found on health store shelves. Later, when I learned that many health food stores had areas in the back of the store or an upstairs mezzanine, which they used for meetings with visiting lecturers, I arranged to have "Doc" make presentations about Food and Drug Administration (FDA) problems, vitamin additions, or other matters of interest. Once or twice, when he could not make it, I served as the speaker. I looked forward to Fridays, as did the retailers, because that was my "free" day when I was able to visit our customers and help them with their problems.

I called the food editor of the *New York Times* to introduce him to the delicious foods and pastries prepared and served by Mr. and Mrs. Sam Brown in their health foods shop and restaurant, *Brownies,* on East 16th Street in Manhattan. It was there, incidentally, that I first met Danny Kaye, Robert Cummings and Eddie Albert, all of whom were regular visitors to *Brownies* whenever they were in town. Through it all, I was able to establish warm and friendly relations with our customers; some of these friendships have survived until today.

Beginning during my second year with the company, I was part of a small contingent of Balanced Foods personnel that staffed our booth at the industry's annual convention, held either in Las Vegas or in Orlando, Florida. There I met some of our out-of-town customers and was able to cement the relationships we had established over the phone.

During this time, I came to respect Sam Reiser's sharp intelligence. He never discouraged me from developing a large number of projects with our customers. He realized early on that I was strengthening customer interest and thereby increasing our business. As long as I adhered to his schedule of order-taking, he decided, quite correctly, that I functioned more effectively unimpeded. I always kept in mind that it was he who had first suggested my joining the staff, and it pleased me to realize that I was vindicating his judgment. While this remained an unspoken understanding between us, I made sure to keep him fully informed in advance of any innovations I planned to undertake.

Despite these positive developments, there were still "glass ceilings" which I could not break through. During my separate conferences with Sam Reiser and "Doc," I was made privy to a considerable amount of information relating to the company's growth plans. However, I was never invited to attend the periodic lunch meetings the three partners held to discuss overall policy. I felt quite confident that the knowledge I was acquiring about the company's operation would have enabled me to make a constructive contribution to those meetings. When I raised the question with Sam, he informed me that all major decisions had to be made by unanimous vote of the partners, and since there was not such unanimity about inviting me to the meetings, I remained on the outside. Deep down, however, I felt it was a question of underestimating a woman's potential.

The main obstacle to the partners' expressing their appreciation for my contribution was Sam's older brother, Will. He became increasingly disturbed by my growing influence within the organization, particularly by my relationship with the other two partners and by my growing impact on our customers. The only way he had of expressing that feeling was by utilizing his veto power, and he did so whenever he could. Perhaps if I had been a man, I would not have appeared so threatening to him.

Another issue that came up was that of my wages. I had agreed that, since I was learning on the job, I would start at the same salary I had been receiving at my not-for-profit job. As soon as my work showed improvement, I was to receive a raise. I waited until the quality of my contribution to the company was quite obvious, but I was put off with the statement that financial circumstances did not permit a significant increase. I had learned that the firm had been started with a loan from the Reisers' father and that for many years, all profits had been ploughed back into the business. So I waited before I asked for and finally got an increase in pay. Then I asked for and obtained raises for my helpers. This turned out to be the way to improve everybody's wages, and I became a one-woman negotiating committee—a position in which I had a great deal of experience. While I was happy to be able to do this for other employees, there seemed to be no possibility of advancement for me. In effect, I had hit a wage-and-role ceiling.

BY THE LATE 1950s, the health foods industry was developing at a much faster pace. Both the giant food industry, which objected to our opposition to food additives, and the American Medical Association (AMA), which resented what they perceived as the threat posed by preventive medicine and vitamin supplements, were urging the Food and Drug Administration (FDA) to rein in this upstart industry. In December, 1960, government agents, using a 1948 legal decision that broadened the definition of labeling to include any written material made available by a merchant in order to sell a specific product, moved into the Balanced Foods warehouse and seized two books from the shelves, Dr. D.C. Jarvis's *Folk Medicine,* and his *Arthritis and Folk Medicine,* along with several bottles of Sterling Cider Vinegar and Honey. They claimed that the fact that the books referred to the preparations by name constituted "labeling." It should be kept in mind that this was taking place in the warehouse of a distributor!

The FDA brought suit against Balanced Foods, claiming that the proximity of the book *Folk Medicine* to the vinegar constituted a mislabeled drug. Attorney Milton Bass was retained to represent the firm. The court ruled in favor of the FDA, but the ruling was overturned by the chief justice of the Court of Appeals when the company was able to prove that it had sold the book for at least two years before it sold the vinegar product. In addition, it had sold about 7,000 copies of the book at two dollars each and only 1,200 bottles of the vinegar preparation at 38 cents each. Besides, there were many other food items placed on the same shelves for shipping convenience. I was a witness at the trial. I saw the judge smile when he heard the statistics and the location of the seized goods. As for the courtroom audience, they laughed out loud and had to be gaveled to silence. However, this was no laughing matter; if the government had won, it would have been illegal for health food stores to sell books that mentioned specific products. During the 1960s, "Big Brother," in the form of the FDA, was illegally "bugging" health food retailers and manufacturers and recording their conversations.

In 1960, THE SAME YEAR in which Balanced Foods was battling the FDA, my son Bob was clashing with the authorities at the Bronx High School of Science while completing his studies there. He and about a dozen of his fellow students refused to sign the special loyalty oath that was then being used by order of the New York City Board of Education. The students were threatened with the loss of their diplomas if they persisted. This, they were told, would prevent them from being accepted by any college. More than half of his fellow objectors gave in at the insistence of their parents and signed. Bob asked for my advice, and I suggested that he use his own judgment, whatever the consequences. He did not sign.

I then went to the American Civil Liberties Union (ACLU) and spoke to Helen Buttenweiser, a highly respected civil liberties attorney. She represented the rebellious students at a Board of Education hearing and succeeded in persuading the Board to eliminate the oath. As a result, from that point on, no one would be called upon to sign it. Bob received his diploma with honors at the graduation ceremony held in the beautiful Loews Paradise Theatre on Grand Concourse in the Bronx. After the graduation, we celebrated at Krum's, our favorite ice cream parlor located nearby. I was very proud of my son.

A FEW YEARS LATER, Dr. Schiff offered me a position as head of a new division, Vitamins for Chiropractors. He had observed the rapid increase of Balanced Foods' sales of his product and had attributed it to my work with the customers. Since he was a man of both integrity and good business sense, he discussed the matter first with Sam Reiser, who was well aware of my feelings of frustration. Sam told him that he would be most unhappy to see me leave, but that only I could make the decision.

It was the summer of 1962. After the industry convention, which was held in July, I moved into Penn South, a brand new union-sponsored cooperative housing development in the Chelsea section of Manhattan. Then I started my job with the Schiff Company in Moonachie, New Jersey—hardly an example of moving near where you work!

Once again, with the assistance of my bakery-owner friend, Herman Cherry, I recommended a replacement for me at Balanced Foods. After she was hired, I worked with her for a week, introducing her to the customers. This proved very helpful, since, after nine mutually productive years, the customers might not have been inclined to adjust very easily to my successor.

Dr. Schiff operated one of the oldest and most respected natural vitamin manufacturing facilities in the industry. He was a courtly gentleman, probably in his early 60s. He harbored a genuine belief in the value of his product and a keen awareness of the developments of this burgeoning health foods lifestyle. He also treated women with respect and consideration, a characteristic I genuinely appreciated.

In my discussions with my new employer before I assumed my unfamiliar responsibilities, I learned that Dr. Schiff had attracted quite a following among chiropractors who were recommending his vitamins to their patients, either under the brand name or under a private label. He believed that, using this group as a nucleus, we would be able to interest a larger group of alternative physicians in the value of vitamin supplements. It sounded both plausible and challenging—two words that had become integral parts of my employment vocabulary. I was to be answerable only to him or his brother-in-law and partner, Phil Pollack. I would have a free hand in planning strategy. From my study of the accumulated files, and by reviewing the available statistics and speaking with doctors, I was able to determine that our presence at conventions would be the best way to obtain a more accurate view of the situation we were facing. I therefore took a booth at the New York State chiropractors' convention and was introduced by friends and supporters to both officials and attendees.

I was disappointed to learn that most chiropractors—like other business people—were only interested in what I had to sell them because of the amount of profit it would produce. Natural vitamins had become just one additional building block in the structure of their businesses. It had been naïve of me to think otherwise. It was the health foods retailers who were the exception.

If my new approach placed a higher premium on profitability, it also gave equal prominence to two factors I regarded as important: efficiency and ethical practices.

There was a disturbing factor in my new job. At the health foods conventions, I had been able to spend evenings chatting with interested customers over good food and a drink. Here, as at most conventions, the convention stay was usually part of the visitors' vacations, and they wanted to have fun and carouse after their booth time was over. The great majority of attendees were men; the few women present were mostly office employees accompanying their salespeople to help cover their booths and they were, in the main, not included in the evening festivities. I was invited by several chiropractors to join the conviviality, but after one or two efforts, it seemed wiser to confine my contacts to the booth or to an early breakfast. The organization dinner and an occasional evening meal with a sober customer were my only after-booth encounters with the group.

Through word of mouth, mailings, ads and articles by Dr. Schiff and other important figures in chiropractic journals, as well as through lectures and conventions, I worked hard to build the division. We had a superior product, growing interest in it, and an increasing number of customers—and so the business grew. Our customers were a mixed group, including both would-be physicians and chiropractors who believed strongly in their own methodology, but it was difficult to establish relationships that were both personal and still somewhat detached. I began to long for my friends in the health foods industry.

Several years later, a then recently organized vitamin company in California, Plus Products, designed a line of vitamins that included an exciting protein powder called "Tiger's Milk," along with a number of distinctive formulas. It was sponsored by one of the most popular natural vitamin writers of the period, Adelle Davis, who is still held in high regard. It was owned and operated by two brothers (the reader may begin to think that this fraternal component is a necessary ingredient of the vitamin industry), and the Ingoldsbys were looking for an Eastern representative to supplement their distributors' efforts. Someone recommended me, and in the spring of 1966, Jim Ingoldsby called, inviting me to an interview. Before I went, I checked with Eugene Schiff to see if he could place me in the direct line of his business. There were no vacancies, but he did offer me a handsome raise if I would stay. However, I was eager to be back with the retailers, and I politely turned him down.

The Ingoldsbys greeted me warmly, showed me their plant and, without much ado, Jim said bluntly, "We're two of the new guys on the block. We think we have an attractive, honest line. We're 3,000 miles away from a very good market in the East.

You're there. We think you can make a difference. Of course, we'll help all we can, but we won't butt in. Do you want to try?" I answered, "Yes." It sounded like a perfect job and it very nearly was.

Jim was the senior partner. He was short, about five-foot-seven, and slender and energetic. He took care of the business end. His brother, Art, was a big man, well-built and possessing a booming laugh. He was the creative partner. The three of us worked together very well. Art and I planned the participation in conventions; Art introduced new items in their small cosmetic line, bought the Steiff tigers that we offered as prizes, and conjured up other gifts. When I ran a Tiger's Milk window-dressing contest, he helped me choose the winners. (I was pleasantly surprised to discover the originality and skills that our customers possessed.) I contributed an exciting Tiger's Milk shopping bag.

I arranged to bring Adelle Davis east for several lectures in her honor. She often added to her prepared presentation a section in which she pointed out the dangers posed by the newly proposed FDA regulations. On June 18, the FDA had announced hearings scheduled for December to consider instituting new regulations which could very well strangle the still-growing health foods industry, at least 30% of which consisted of vitamins. The proposed regulations provided, among other items, that no store could sell, without a prescription, any product containing more than 150% of the new Recommended Dietary Allowance (RDA) prepared by the Food and Nutrition Board of the National Research Council, a government agency. This was an updated version of the former Minimum Daily Requirements (MDR) that were to be used as informational guidelines for planning by scientists, the industry and the general public.

Starting in 1962 and for the next 14 years, the industry fought for its very existence—beginning with its appeal of the unreasonable choice of the hearing examiner assigned to conduct the hearings and continuing through the multiple decisions and appeals to the courts. There was always the Damoclean sword

hanging over its head. Concurrently, the National Nutritional Foods Association (NNFA) was conducting a struggle in Congress, the original source of the authority governing the regulatory agency. On one of the industry's representatives' special trips to Washington, they brought with them a million signatures supporting their position—the largest such action since the Vietnam war. Finally, in April, 1976, President Gerald Ford signed a landmark nutritional rights bill that embodied all the industry's recommended provisions. Milton Bass, the industry's attorney, called it "the greatest victory for the nutrition industry ever achieved, protecting freedom of choice for millions." Included among its eight listed provisions were:
- That the FDA may not establish maximum potencies for safe vitamins and minerals.
- That an individual consumer can decide how much of a vitamin or mineral he or she desired.
- That the FDA cannot determine how much of a vitamin or mineral an individual needed.

Adelle Davis and I often ate together when she came east for her lectures. She was a passionate believer in the ideas she put forth. She always carried packets of Tiger's Milk with her, pouring the powder into the extra glass she requested from the waiter and adding skim milk to it. She was sure it was superior to any comparable product. Unlike me and so many other lecturers I have observed through the years, she was remarkably calm before delivering a lecture. Just a year earlier, in 1965, she had had her fourth or fifth book, *Let's Get Well*, published by Harcourt Brace and World. Like its predecessors, it was an instant best-seller.

I attribute much of Ms. Davis's success to the fact that she tried to work with the medical profession rather than opposing it. *Let's Get Well* was dedicated to the "hundreds of wonderful doctors whose research made this book possible." Although the AMA was one of the strongest opponents of the nutrition industry, a growing number of doctors were beginning to acknowledge the helpfulness of vitamin supplements, and they were among those who flocked to hear and support Ms. Davis.

She often spoke to me about how one doctor, then another, following her endorsements, had suggested vitamins to his or her patients and had expressed deep gratitude to her for the results. Her visits east constituted a huge triumph for the industry.

In order to keep my employers informed of my activities, I dictated detailed weekly reports describing every visit I made to retailers and distributors alike. I could not be sure that they were ever fully read. In fact, when I spoke on the phone to Jim Ingoldsby, regarding a trip I had just made, he often sounded as if he did not know what I was talking about. Still, I felt that this was part of my job and, in addition, it enabled me to keep a record of my activities for follow-up purposes.

In each of the three years during which I represented Plus Products, I visited the company's site in Los Angeles in order to help prepare and design the products catalog. This offered me an opportunity to renew our relationships. It also provided the brothers with an opportunity to show their hospitality. They would urge me to attend the theatrical performances at the Dorothy Chandler Pavilion and they took me to some of the finest, though not necessarily the fanciest, Mexican and Chinese restaurants. I must confess that this was one of the reasons I looked forward to these annual trips. One year, they sent me off to Catalina Island for an extra week of vacation. On my third visit, they offered me the position of national director, which was new for them, but which they then considered necessary. I graciously declined. I had no intention of spending all my time traveling.

As stores grew and customers expressed increased confidence in their retailers' choices, customized labels were coming very much in vogue. The customers' trust would be heightened if the retailer selected the finest formulations of the highest quality. This accounted for the interest expressed by successful manufacturers in this phase of sales.

It was against this background that, at the 1969 NNFA convention, Phil Pollack pleaded with me to return to Schiff to work in their new private label department. They had acquired both the program and the director who had been running it for many years. They wanted me to join the department, to become completely familiar with it and then to take over when the current director, who was constantly threatening to retire, actually did. I was assured and reassured that, if hired, I would only supersede him when he was ready to leave.

Meanwhile, the Ingoldsbys had selected a sales manager with whom I knew I would not be able to get along. He was pompous, extravagant and more intent on talking than on working. I therefore accepted the Schiff offer, which would permit me to continue to work with my retailer friends in a congenial atmosphere and with a future ahead of me that fit my needs.

Fred Frankel, who ran the private label sector, was the most unlikely health food industry operative I had ever encountered. He was heavy-set, could not complete a sentence without profanity and both drank and smoked. He always expressed his opinions freely—and in expletives. He immediately reacted negatively to my presence, accusing both his employers and me of wanting to get rid of him. He admitted that he had often talked about leaving, but claimed that these were only threats intended to enable him to "get my [expletive] way." On the other hand, he was a hard worker, fulfilled his commitments diligently and was loyal to his customers. I tried very hard to reach an amicable arrangement with him, but he was also very stubborn. I therefore had to work around him. I was careful never to criticize him to our customers, who expressed their wonder at how I was able to work with him. Some years later, while writing an order, he died of a heart attack.

Eugene Schiff was in poor health and was participating less and less in the company's daily activities. As soon as I returned, I noticed the vast difference between his involvement when I was first at the plant and now. Phil Pollack, whose sister was married to Schiff, was much younger and a comparative newcomer to the business. On every level, he was light years behind his brother-in-law. Among other weaknesses, he was indecisive and lacked a detailed knowledge of the business.

When Eugene Schiff died in 1969, many of the company's top supervisors began to seek a way out. One of them, Bob Krall, whom Schiff had brought east from a midwestern university a few years earlier, suggested that a few of us start our own company.

AFTER TWO YEARS spent mulling over this possibility, six of us decided to take the plunge. Our group included Krall, who was designated president of the overall enterprise; a friend of his, Jerry Gaunt, who was a distinguished biology professor from England's Oxford University; Felix Jehle, chief of research and development, who had had 17 years' experience in that department at Squibb Products; Fred Stewart, supervisor of production; Michael Platzman, our attorney and a former clerk to Supreme Court Justice Louis Brandeis, with considerable trial and business experience, and me, as president of our new brand, Synergy Plus.

Through Michael's efforts, we were able to raise enough capital to rent a fully-equipped facility in Union, New Jersey, which contained comfortably furnished offices, complete with handsome desks, credenzas and bookcases. We managed to secure a satisfactory long-term lease, to purchase the essential raw materials and packaging equipment and to staff the production facility and clerical offices. I worked far into the night putting together the Synergy Plus product catalog. Felix and I had fun concocting names like "Pep Power" for our protein powder, "Child Love" for our children's vitamin, and "Synergy Plus" as our vitamin brand. Four of us—Felix Jehle, Fred Stewart, Michael Platzman and I—not only did all the work, but we had the contacts, both within and outside the industry, that enabled us to start and then continue what was to become a highly successful business.

Since I was the only partner who had connections with the retailers, I prepared a letter, in consultation with my partners and with our advertising agency, in which I explained why we had gone into business and introducing the principals of our new company to potential customers. It was very well received and produced many encouraging responses.

During our first year, Dr. Jerry Gaunt died of liver cancer. Bob Krall, who had the original idea and was the first president of our overall company, the International Vitamin Company, had done nothing but call meetings and issue redundant instructions, which, in many instances, had already been fulfilled. By unanimous vote, he was replaced by Felix Jehle. I remained the president of Synergy Plus.

The four remaining partners worked very well together during the seventeen years in which we were in business. Felix, our president, was a brilliant scientist with a tremendous knowledge of the intricacies of the vitamin formulations. He was kind and gentle and was able to quickly extinguish the sudden outbursts and frequent disagreements engendered by seemingly insoluble problems. Michael was an exceptional lawyer. Fred had supervised workers on an assembly line for 25 years. And I had close relationships with the retailers and many of the distributors. In addition, despite our political differences, we were all highly ethical. We respected one another and appreciated the special capabilities we each brought to the table. I was the only woman in the group and the only female president in the industry who had attained that position without either inheriting or marrying into it. I cannot remember one occasion during our association when my gender was a cause for denigration or disrespect.

Among the many writers in the industry, we worked most closely with Carlton Fredericks, who was far ahead of his time. We sponsored his program on WOR radio and recommended him as a lecturer at the annual conventions. His work on estrogen and cancer constituted an early warning of the many revelations which were to come later.

Felix, in consultation with Fredericks, originated the first multiple antioxidant, which we promptly added to our product line. Other products were developed, based on the essential vitamins, and this served to make Synergy an innovative brand that did not have to resort to fad formulations. Our first successful item was Pep Power, an excellent protein drink. I later ran a national recipe contest, and the resulting cookbook was widely distributed.

Our private label served as the special niche to enter the industry, which by then had accumulated a plethora of both major and minor brands. Our reputation helped us grow, even though we were founded during a recession in the early '70s. We were warmly welcomed by our friends in the industry. Henry Foner, by then the president of the Fur, Leather and Machine Workers Union, offered our formulations to his union members at special prices with a unique "FLM" imprint and received an excellent response.

I was 59 years old when we launched our enterprise in 1972; Michael was a few years older and the other two a few years younger. Even though we had made a great deal of progress, a decade later, we were still a small, quality business. We began to think about turning our company over to family members, but no one was interested. Hence, we waited a few years and then seriously sought a buyer. We did not want to sell to just any company; even under these circumstances, we still maintained our high standards.

Several large mainstream food companies, realizing that there was "gold in them thar vitamins," were hunting for possible additions, but they wanted bigger companies. Smaller buyers were not prepared to pay what we were asking. We finally found a bulk-producing manufacturer who did a large export business and was looking for quality brand names. We had two superior ones to offer—Synergy Plus and International Vitamin Company. We were in the process of negotiating the deal when our attorney, Michael, became too ill to continue (he died soon afterwards). We had to start over midway, under far less favorable conditions. Although the net proceeds of the sale we finally consummated were far less than we had been previously offered, we were glad when it was all over. Our company was sold in 1989.

Part VI
Retirement

Chapter 13
Return to Community Work

I officially retired in 1989 at the age of 76, when we sold our vitamin business. Although I had received several attractive offers, I had not decided what I would do next. I certainly did not want to undertake full-time work. I decided to relax for six months, and then....

In the meantime, I took a trip to Alaska with my friends, Al and Marsha Smith. I returned home in time to listen to and exchange views with Brian Lehrer, host of the new and exciting WNYC news program, "On the Line." At the same time, I was slowly getting rid of the last remnants of the pressure induced by my former position. A Penn South neighbor informed me that it was possible to obtain tickets for excellent concerts and performances of both Broadway and off-Broadway shows at the nearby Hudson Guild Fulton Senior Center. While completing my membership application, I had a conversation with the Center's program director, who urged me to participate in its activities.

After working for a while with the Center's membership and advisory committees, I reluctantly accepted the post of president of its Volunteer Senior Association. There I inaugurated a many-faceted project called "A Home Away from Home," aimed at making the Center more inviting by soliciting and exhibiting paintings from our artist members and prints from various museums, as well as plants from the neighborhood florists and comfortable chairs from residents who no longer needed them. I also utilized a bulletin board that listed the Center's varied events and secured the willing assistance of the art teacher to keep it engaging. It told of art classes, craft groups, lectures and outings. We invited outside speakers to discuss current issues of interest. In order to encourage our Latino members to join in our activities, we recruited translators from among our members. In 1992, at its annual dinner, the Guild honored me with its John Lovejoy Elliott Award, named after the Guild's founder, as the Outstanding Senior of the Year.

Then a member of the Center's social action committee invited me to accompany her to a citywide meeting of the Joint Public Affairs Committee (JPAC), a grassroots organization that helps older people work together to become more effective advocates of their own interests. The stimulating discussions, the "can-do" atmosphere that prevailed there, and the ever-present emphasis on action, not just words, all served to convince me that this would be a worthwhile pursuit for me. As soon as my term as president of the Center's association was over, I plunged head-long into JPAC.

At one of the early JPAC meetings I attended, I met Arthur Elliot, with whom I had worked in my first job in the Emergency Relief Bureau back in the early 1930s. He had been an active member of the union and had attended many of our picnics and other social events. He had become an effective participant in a number of community organizations, including both JPAC and the Congress of Senior Citizens. He welcomed me with open arms. At the same meeting, I renewed my acquaintance with Max Manes, who had been a leader of the rank-and-file of the Hat, Cap and Millinery Workers Union when I was running the fund-raising bazaars. He and his co-workers had made an impressive contribution to the success of those events. Since then, Max had played a leading role in a number of social issue campaigns and, more recently, in senior activities. It was he who organized Seniors for Adequate Social Security (SASS). His experience in both JPAC and the Congress of Senior Citizens was invaluable. We were both delighted to meet again.

I also renewed my friendship with a woman who had worked closely with my mother in the Emma Lazarus clubs in the Bronx. Our reunion was particularly moving because it brought back so many warm memories. Until her illness prevented her from doing so, she remained a regular attendee at JPAC's meetings.

Another old friend I met there was Henry Foner, who frequently accompanied his wife, Lorraine, to the JPAC meetings, at which she represented the Brooklyn Chapter of the Older Women's League (OWL). The reader will recall that he had twice earlier entered these pages in his role as a leader of the Furriers' Union, first, in connection with the union's dental clinic, and later in helping his union members benefit from the resources of the Synergy Plus vitamin enterprise. I was pleased to note that he was more active than ever, using his skills on behalf of a variety of organizations. Once again, there was an enthusiastic reunion, tinged with reminiscences.

Organizationally speaking, I was home again!

I became a regular member of JPAC's advisory committee with the special responsibility of preparing papers and providing testimony at hearings on health care, Medigap insurance (policies designed to supplement Medicare benefits), prescription drug coverage, and a number of other issues vital to seniors. My work at JPAC gave me the same type of satisfaction I had derived from my trade union activities—the opportunity to evaluate issues, plan actions, make our voices heard, and most important of all, obtain results. I shared chairing the committee with Sylvia Bassoff, the courageous leader of the disabled who was largely responsible for obtaining Access-a-Ride, that unique New York City bus system for seniors and the disabled. Still later, I was appointed the only lay member of the advisory committee of the New York City Commissioner for the Department of Aging.

One of JPAC's most effective activities was and continues to be its annual delegation trek to the state capital in Albany. There we meet with the leaders of both legislative bodies and seek to convince them to retain and expand existing senior programs. We also seek their support for additional legislation on housing, health insurance, prescription drug coverage, nursing home resident protection and a number of broader community issues. Appointments are made in advance with the key legislative leaders, and detailed position papers are prepared to help educate the participants. On the bus trip to the capital, they have an opportunity to digest and discuss the papers so that they may present the issues convincingly to the legislators. Upon arrival in Albany, we break up into delegations of from five to seven members each and each group meets with at least three different legislators. Between meetings, briefings are held to review results and prepare for the next encounter.

During my third such trip, everything had gone as planned— our JPAC staff had meticulously arranged all the details and each delegation had had its share of vocal and eloquent participants. However, I was both disappointed and frustrated to note that some delegation members were hesitant to speak up, while others strayed from our agenda and discussed extraneous subjects. It was then that the idea occurred to me that what our members needed was more in-depth knowledge of the issues, more practice in delivering focused statements, and a greater amount of confidence building.

At the next advisory committee meeting, I raised these concerns and pointed out that they applied not only to the Albany delegations, but also to other of the organization's activities. I insisted that there was a need to develop greater advocacy skills among our senior members and that the answer might lie in conducting multisession classes in both advocacy and leadership. At this point, a committee member spoke up: "We've tried that before and it didn't work."

"Let's try it again!" I responded. After an animated discussion, the proposal was adopted. A committee was selected to explore the idea further and I accepted the responsibility of chairing it.

In the course of developing the project, we met frequently with JPAC director Caryn Resnick, who welcomed the idea enthusiastically. We also consulted with David Stern, the executive director of JPAC's parent body, the Jewish Association for Services to the Aged (JASA), as well as with Robert Stephens, the training director of New York City's Department for the Aging (DFTA) and, from Hunter College's Brookdale Center of the Aging, deputy director Rick Moody and Sam Sadin, one of the original organizers of the Center. We met, too, with legislators, labor leaders and senior activists and "picked the brains" of such public figures as Brian Lehrer of Station WNYC and Gail Collins of the *New York Times*. These meetings had the additional advantage of providing us with a corps of experts whom we could later call to help staff our teaching body – which many of them generously did, working *pro bono.*

We still had many hurdles to overcome, but after about a year, we were able to hammer out all the details. When we were through, we had designed what came to be known as the Institute for Senior Action (IFSA)—a 10-week training course for about 25 students, to be held twice a year and consisting of two classes held one day each week. The list of subjects included:

> "Getting to Know You" – An Introductory Session.
> City, State and National Bugets and Legislative Processes.
> Learning Senior Issues.
> Senior Entitlements.
> Working Intergenerationally.
> How to Run an Effective Meeting.
> Volunteerism and Mentoring.
> Writing Skills and Techniques.
> The Media: A Tool for Social Action.
> Public Speaking with Confidence.
> Issue Analysis for Public Presentation.
> Techniques of Social Action.
> Organizing in a Multicultural Environment.
> Voter Registration and Outreach.

One of our major goals was to reflect the rich ethnic, cultural and organizational differences in New York City. Our first class, which began in March, 1994, consisted mainly of advisory committee members. By the time we celebrated our 10th anniversary in June, 2004, we had graduated more than four hundred and eighty trained, self-confident leaders. They represented 332 organizations and more than half of them came from minority populations.

Our graduates have spread throughout metropolitan New York and serve as a self-renewing reservoir of extraordinary activists. As a result of lowering the minimum age to 55, half of our students are now 65 or younger. They represent senior centers, trade union retiree groups, community boards, political parties, grandparent coalitions, Y's, settlement houses, churches, synagogues, mosques, the disabled, ethnic groups, OWL, SAGE, AARP, the Gray Panthers, and more.

In our effort to achieve diversity, we have cemented our bonds with New York City's trade union movement, many of whose new members come from minority groups. The unions have proven to be fertile ground from which we receive potential advocates. Their older members bring a great deal of experience to the classes, and their presence has had both an informative and an invigorating effect. For their younger members, the classes provide needed and greatly appreciated information in their efforts to improve their conditions.

We have been able to establish and maintain contact with a number of union retiree groups who wisely absorb graduates into leadership positions. The retirees' organization of District Council 37 of the American Federation of State, County and Municipal Employees (AFSCME), led by its president, Stuart Leibowitz, has sent the largest number of members to the program—42 in all. Local 237 of the International Brotherhood of Teamsters (IBT) has referred 31 students and, when we faced an emergency, the local generously made available the use of its meeting hall for our classes. The director of Local 237's retirees' organization, Nancy True, and the editor of its publication, Donna Ristorucci, both take great pride in the relationship and in the benefits it has brought to their members. According to Ms. True:

> "Our members usually speak loudly, but they advocate even more loudly and clearly after they take the IFSA course. They learn not only from the excellent teachers, but also from their fellow students who come from so many different places, but all of whom have the same goal—a better life for all."

Local 1180 of the Communication Workers of America (CWA) has been responsible for 14 graduates. Other unions that have participated in the program include 1199/SEIU, the United Federation of Teachers (UFT), Local 259 of the United Automobile Workers (UAW), UNITE, representing workers in the garment trades, and Local 6 of the Hotel Employees and Restaurant Employees (HERE). (The two last-named organizations have since merged to become UNITE-HERE.) The Coalition of Black Trade Unionists (CBTU) has also been represented.

Despite the marked differences in the students' backgrounds, ethnicity, places of birth, education, economic condition and often in tactical approach, the classes have been remarkably harmonious. The students have formed relationships that have continued after the classes end. They are united by a common desire to work for a fairer, more equitable society. Since our graduates are our best recruiters, registration has continued to grow, and as of this writing, there is even a waiting list.

We have received numerous requests from all over the country for help in establishing similar institutes. Since we do not have the resources to send trained representatives, we have prepared a manual, *Tool Kit for Advocacy*, written by several of our graduates and jointly edited by our present director and myself. It is a comprehensive compilation of "how-to" suggestions, including class content, role-playing exercises, graphics and resources, and it has received wide acclaim from its many users. We have also completed an oral history embracing the experiences of thirty of our outstanding graduates, which we presented as an exhibit to an enthusiastic audience at our tenth anniversary celebration. It will also be displayed at senior centers and union halls.

One of our major sources of pride has been the number of specific pieces of legislation that have been passed as a result of the activities of our graduates and our coalition partners. In 2001, for example, the Welfare Rights Initiative (WRI), our intergenerational partner at Hunter College, which helps single mothers on relief obtain college degrees, succeeded in getting a bill passed by the New York State legislature and signed by the governor that permitted the substitution of college courses and internships for workfare as a requirement for continued eligibility for welfare assistance. Statistics show that almost 90% of single mothers who graduate from college are able to leave the welfare rolls permanently. Similarly, the Grandparents for Children's Rights, after having been advised by the so-called "experts" that they would never succeed, were able to achieve special rights for grandparents and grandchildren. Brigitte Castellano, an Institute graduate and founder of the Grandparents for Children's Rights, wrote to me:

> As you know, the Governor recently signed the Grandparent Caregiver Rights Act into law. We have been lobbying for this legislation for two years and were told that such legislation would never be enacted in New York State. We were successful, Dorothy, because we had you as a role model. The IFSA course that I was privileged to attend taught me all the elements that I needed to advocate successfully.

We have chosen as our slogan "Learn, then Act," because it describes precisely what we attempt to do. We train and then send our graduates back to their organizations where they can put their newly-acquired knowledge to good use. Our formula is to work together for change and mutual betterment. Many of our graduates elect to devote their energies to JPAC itself and its many committees.

At an IFSA graduation ceremony held in the late '90s, David Stern, director of JASA, walked in with a visitor, Martin Edelman, a JASA Board member. We later learned that Mr. Edelman had expressed interest in the Institute. David thought that the best way he could learn about it was by attending an IFSA event. Fortunately, we were about to graduate our eighth IFSA class.

The two men sat in the back. When we urged them to come to the dais, they explained that Mr. Edelman had to leave early and that they would prefer to sit where they could depart without causing any disruption. Both left quietly after an hour and a half. A short time afterward, David returned, smiling broadly. He informed us that Mr. Edelman had been so fascinated by the proceedings and by what they demonstrated about the work of IFSA that he had written a $10,000 check for the Institute in order to encourage its continuation and growth.

That same year, Martin Edelman was the honoree at JASA's Annual Gala Dinner. He paid for a table for current graduates and made IFSA's advocacy training the theme of his acceptance speech. When he asked the table's occupants to stand, they did so to considerable applause; he then called for a special "Thank you" for IFSA's founder. Needless to say, we were grateful for both the contribution and the added stature it brought to the program.

No story about our Institute for Senior Action would be complete without an expression of deep appreciation to the 81 dedicated teachers who have taught classes and then returned to teach some more. Many of them have been with us for a number of terms and some for all of them. They have helped to empower our remarkably committed seniors while exchanging ideas with them.

Two who have been there throughout the entire 20 semesters are Rose Dobrof, founder of the Brookdale Center on Aging, and John Lawniczak, director of government relations for the Coalition of Health Services Research. Rose, whose classes I attend whenever I can, injects new data into each session. As she has said: "IFSA is magnificent testimony to its founder, Dorothy Epstein, and it reflects also the fidelity of the five-hundred participants in the classes to the cause of social betterment. They are wonderful people, and it is a joy to be with them—and to learn from them." As for John, he comes all the way from Washington just to teach the class. He has the demanding task of making federal legislation and the budget understandable in one session. "I wouldn't miss it for the world," he says. "The students are so eager and ready to learn! I'm never bored—and I hope they aren't either."

One of our original teachers, who taught "Public Speaking with Confidence," had to leave the program when his new job took him out of the city. The acting provost at Hunter College secured an equally talented substitute. When the original teacher returned to the city two years later and was prepared to resume teaching the class, his successor simply refused to give it up! As our JPAC coalition work widens its circle of influence, the breadth of teacher possibilities also broadens. Since the word of our success is spread by our devoted alumni, we have no problem replacing instructors when the situation demands it.

As for me, I never cease being inspired by the quality of our extraordinary student body. Each new coalition partner yields new recruits who come fully prepared to learn, utilize their lunch hours to get petitions signed, join picket lines and exchange experiences.

And most of them, regardless of their background, acquire as early as the first class—"Getting to Know You"—an ability to carry on discussions without rancor and to adjust to the many role-playing parts that are an integral aspect of their learning process. This alone is quite amazing, because, while the older students have had considerable experience, the so-called "younger" ones, from 55 to 65, are coming to grips with many problems for the first time. Meanwhile, some of our graduates have been able to persuade the leaders of their organizations to enroll as well, so that they, too, can obtain the necessary skills and teach them to others.

Our graduates are truly remarkable. In spite of "bad days" and personal illnesses, they are always ready to help others by working in hospitals, settlement houses and similar institutions. A former nurse works with Alzheimer patients; one student walked a neighbor facing eviction through the legal steps necessary to prevent that event from happening. The Institute's experience has demonstrated conclusively that knowledge and its proper use instills confidence, strengthens morale and achieves effective results.

We have been indeed fortunate that JPAC's current director, Amy West Poley, who was our first paid IFSA director, has had a deep and abiding devotion to both the project itself and its students. She and her staff, as well as IFSA'S current director, Molly Sager, are all creative and hard-working young people who have contributed greatly to the project's success.

Through the years, I have never forgotten that it was at the Hudson Guild that I first became aware of JPAC and its many productive activities. I was delighted to learn that the Guild, which is undergoing a renovation and modernization of its facilities, is setting aside a room for IFSA's classes.

Since retiring in 1989, the years with JPAC, as well as those with Hunter College described in the next chapter, have been among the most fulfilling and productive of my long life. I have discovered that, despite the difficult world in which we live—the hunger, the illiteracy and the endless wars—there are overwhelming numbers of decent people in the world who want only to live at peace with their neighbors and to work at satisfying and productive jobs.

One evening in 1934, after visiting my home relief clients, I had a dream. That dream was partially realized when we won the right to organize into unions and secured Social Security, unemployment insurance, Medicare and Medicaid. However, every one of these gains is being eroded, bit by bit. I am convinced that the perseverance of the IFSA graduates and of so many more like them will some day help make my dream become a permanent reality.

Many public officials have been highly supportive of our efforts. The list includes: Congressional representatives Charles Rangel and Jerrold Nadler; Manhattan borough presidents past and present, Ruth Messinger and C. Virginia Fields; former Brooklyn borough president Howard Golden; Bronx borough president Adolfo Carrion, Jr.; New York City Council Speaker Gifford Miller and Council members Christina Quinn and Margarita Lopez; New York State Senators Liz Krueger and Tom Duane; and New York State Assembly members Richard Gottfried and Deborah Glick; and many others.

In 1999, when the level of my blood pressure and the effects of multiple medications were preventing me from functioning effectively, I heeded my doctor's advice and resigned my post at IFSA. I did so at a deeply moving assemblage of JPAC members, IFSA graduates, coalition associates and a large number

of the legislators whose friendship and support we had cultivated. The occasion also marked the 10th semester of IFSA and
the launching of the *Dorothy Epstein/IFSA Legacy Award*. My
voice was choked with emotion, pleasure and appreciation, as I
thanked all the wonderful people present. Equally as affecting
as the many plaques, citations and proclamations from organizations and legislators were the warm and eloquent greetings
spontaneously inscribed in an album circulated during the event
and handed to me when it was over.

As I sat listening to the "eulogies," I had the strange sense of
being a *voyeur* at my own memorial. However, it was far better
to be alive and present. Too often, these genuine emotional
expressions of respect and love come too late for the person
for whom they are intended to appreciate them. Once again,
I learned how truly wonderful people are and how fortunate I
have been to share their aspirations and achievements.

Someone once wrote (it might even have been me) that there
is no better cure for what ails you than continued activity. It
certainly proved true in my case. A few months after I had had
to curtail my activities, having changed both my doctor and my
medications, I was able to start again—a little less peripatetic,
perhaps, but well enough to continue to explore IFSA's almost
limitless possibilities. I fleetingly considered whether I should
offer to return the plaques tendered to me upon retirement, but
they made such an attractive display on my wall that I quickly
banished the thought.

In May, 2002, the Chelsea Reform Democratic Club (CRDC)
presented me with their first Progressive Community Award
named for the late Esther Smith. It was an honor I deeply
appreciated because I had a great deal of respect for Esther, who
had worked with me at Russian War Relief. In the years that
followed, she was a strong fighter for civil rights and progressive
political action.

Chapter 14
Hunter College, Again

Gertrude Groden, president of the Hunter College Class of 1933, had often expressed her frustration over the failure of the Alumnae (later Alumni) Association to provide her and her classmates with notices of its activities. When she was elected president in the late 1960s, she was determined that our class would become recognized as a vital part of the Association. She instituted annual class meetings, to which all of us were invited, and took the necessary steps to insure that we received all the pertinent information, including invitations to the annual luncheons.

In 1949, the Scholarship and Welfare Fund was established, and it did not take long for Gertrude to become involved in its activities. In 1974, she was invited to join its board and she proceeded to make sure that the Fund became a critical focus of our class's activities. This resolve was strengthened when, two years later, Hunter lost its free tuition.

The first project Gertrude undertook for our class was the establishment of an undergraduate scholarship named for our former class president, Mary Candib, who had recently died. When this was completed successfully within just a few months, Gertrude was encouraged and she proposed to a number of us who had responded to her appeals that each of us launch our own individual scholarships. Up to that point, I had attended our class meetings only infrequently, but I soon became one of Gertrude's most vocal supporters in this new effort. Like my classmates, I was very much upset by the demise of free tuition in the city colleges. For many of us, this had been the "crown jewel" in our collection of Hunter treasures. As a result, when the Scholarship and Welfare Fund added a "Scholars" award providing for the payment of all fees for all four years at the college, our class immediately established one for the Fund's use. For myself, I considered this a logical way of expressing my gratitude for the benefits that free tuition had brought me by helping students like myself enjoy the opportunities I had had.

Largely through Gertrude's zealous efforts, our "depression" class became one of the major contributors to the Scholarship and Welfare Fund's projects, providing the highest number of individual and class scholarships. We all felt a deep sense of loss when Gertrude died just before our seventieth reunion in 2003 after serving as class president for forty years. The last class gift we sponsored was a dormitory scholarship in her name.

In 1985, I visited Hunter for the first time since my graduation. The purpose of my call was to meet the dynamic Donna Shalala, then the president of the college and later Secretary of Health and Human Services in President Clinton's cabinet. I learned that I was to be inducted into the Alumni Hall of Fame. While there, I looked in vain for the venerable neo-Gothic building that had provided our main support in the 1930s. It was gone, having burned down three years after our graduation, and had been replaced by an art deco structure built by the WPA. Two new buildings, recently completed and connected by an overhead bridge, now constituted the center of the school's activities.

Inside the college, I experienced additional shocks of nonrecognition. First, unlike in our days, the interior was painted in cheerful colors. The college's student body was now composed of students from a hundred and forty different countries, more than half of whom came from minority populations. The halls, corridors and elevators were filled with groups of mixed gender, nationality and color, walking, talking and laughing. Like the Class of 1933, many had to work while attending college and therefore required more than four years to complete their studies. All told, it was a pleasant surprise—both visually and emotionally.

During the 1980s, while I was still working at Synergy Plus, I donated a graduate fellowship in nutrition at the college's School of Health Sciences. President Shalala had assured me that the Scholarship and Welfare Fund was on a firm footing and said that the School of Health Sciences needed this kind of assistance. Being a strong believer in nutrition, I readily complied.

At this point, I was invited by the dean of that school to personally present the fellowship award and also to learn more about the school's faculty and students. In 1989, an innovative requirement for the award—that is, the development of a nutrition project that would involve the participation of a community group—was added. This encouraged the school to establish relationships with neighborhood organizations. It also stimulated the publication, in May, 2000, of a booklet recording the school's projects for the decade from 1989 to 1999. I received the first copy on the occasion celebrating the opening of the Health Services Laboratory, which I had helped to equip.

In 1992, at an informal luncheon with the school's students to discuss future fellowships, one of the stouter participants called out, "How about obesity?" Everyone laughed. One person even responded, "All you have to do is eat less!" Assistant Professor Deborah Blocker, who sponsored these regular get-togethers, later told me that that humorous exchange had remained in her mind, and in the Spring, 2001, issue of *The Journal of the American Medical Women's Association*, she had had published an article, "Developing Comprehensive Approaches to the Prevention and Control of Obesity Among Low-Income, Urban African-American Women." It was introduced by an opening statement which read: "Obesity will be the most important public health nutrition concern of the 21st Century." This was hardly an exaggeration, since obesity has now been recognized as a serious problem affecting our nation's health and as the cause of many serious diseases. In fact, it has been estimated that as much as sixty-five percent of our population is overweight.

In cooperation with the school's Nutrition Department, and particularly with its chair, Arlene Spark, we initiated a series of annual Dorothy Epstein Nutrition Lectures which were open to all interested students, faculty members, students from other colleges, and lay persons in cooperating community groups. Our first lecture, on October 16, 2002, was by Balz Frei, president of the Linus Pauling Institute. I have been deeply impressed, not only by the interest in nutrition expressed by the school's students and faculty alike, but also by their genuine concern with what was happening in their community.

At this time, I was also discovering that the lesson my parents had carefully taught me, to give whatever financial assistance I could to organizations and causes that needed money to perform their necessary work, was standing me in good stead. When we sold our vitamin enterprise in 1989, I had an opportunity to make meaningful donations to some of the institutions I had long admired. I also made what was, for me, a crucial decision. Even though it might place in jeopardy the funds for my son's future, I decided to overcome my deep-seated objections and to take advantage of the possibilities offered by the stock market, all the while trying to be as careful as possible. As a result, I placed my share of the proceeds from the sale in the hands of a broker who invested only in socially responsible enterprises and who was aware of my concerns. I chose a 10-year, irrevocable charitable end trust as the best means of achieving my goal. Upon the trust's termination, the principal remaining would go directly to my heirs.

My most significant gift went to Hunter for its very first endowed chair, in Latin American history. I chose that area after considerable discussion with the college's new president, Paul LeClerc, because I felt that the traditional accounts of the history of our Latin American neighbors had been both meager and distorted. My gift brought to Hunter Dr. Margaret E. Crahan, a distinguished scholar of Latin American history who had previously been the Henry R. Luce Professor at Occidental College. Equally important, it aroused fresh interest in the process of establishing chairs as a means of enhancing the college's stature. Many alumni were prompted to contact me to learn about the particulars of such a donation, and, not surprisingly, there are now at least five similarly endowed chairs in art, social work, the sciences and public policy.

Two other major beneficiaries of my trust have been Amnesty International, for its work in Latin America, and the American Civil Liberties Union, with particular emphasis on its efforts to maintain the separation of church and state in our nation's affairs. There were also a number of smaller annual donations to the Children's Defense Fund, the Southern Poverty Law Center, the Linus Pauling Institute, *Jewish Currents* magazine and the Jane Addams Fund of the Women's International League for Peace and Freedom (WILPF).

I also took advantage of the opportunity to participate in a number of organizations and activities that I had been too busy for during my working years: the Friends of the Art Gallery; the Sylvia and Danny Kaye Guild, supporting its dance and theatre activities; and the Symphony Society of Hunter College. I became a pioneer member of the Thomas Hunter Society, whose members provide financial support for the college through bequests, and I am a board member of the college's Scholarship and Welfare Fund.

At President LeClerc's farewell celebration in November, 1993, he awarded me the prestigious President's Medal at an inspirational ceremony. He had previously honored me for my gift of the chair, which was again recognized by then acting president Blanche Blank when the chair was filled. Several years later, in 1998, at its annual luncheon, the Alumni Association presented me with a unique award—truly unique, since it is the only ever awarded—for Outstanding Community Service. In my acceptance speech, I talked of the inspiring history of Hunter graduates' efforts on behalf of the working poor in the neighboring Yorkville section of New York City during the last third of the Nineteenth Century.

In 1870, Hunter had been officially recognized as a normal school for girls. Concerned graduates had begun a kindergarten, taught teenage boys to do carpentry work and other useful occupations, instructed girls in sewing, organized after-school games and established a settlement house which evolved into the Lenox Hill Neighborhood House. They took care of the "latch-key" children of German immigrants when both parents had to work to earn enough to provide for their families. The men were often employed in Yorkville breweries and their wives in storefront cigar factories. To this day, the Lenox Hill Neighborhood House has a clause in its constitution mandating the inclusion of Hunter alumni on its board of directors.

Through my endowed chair's first occupant, Margaret "Meg" Crahan, I became acquainted with the Welfare Rights Initiative (WRI) at Hunter. I had requested her help in finding an effective student advocacy group. At that time, Maureen Lane, who had been one of the star students in Hunter's Human Rights Internship Program, was a leader of the WRI. Maureen and I met, discussed our two groups—JPAC's Institute for Senior Action and the WRI—and concluded that they made a perfect fit. It was agreed that Maureen would conduct the intergenerational class in our course and that one of us in IFSA would prepare the material for an equivalent course in their Leadership Training Class.

Since that time some eight years ago, Maureen and several of her most promising students have taught in every session of the IFSA course to considerable acclaim. We gave them a well-deserved tribute at our tenth year IFSA celebration in June, 2004.

WRI, which consists mainly of single mothers on welfare seeking an academic degree and the independence of a decent job, has shown itself to be a courageous and effective group. As mentioned previously, they succeeded in securing passage by the New York State Legislature of a bill that permitted the substitution of college courses and internships for workfare in qualifying for welfare assistance. Prior to its passage, thousands of welfare mothers attending the City University of New York (CUNY) had been forced to leave school because of their impossible workloads. WRI's success has validated a belief expressed by many of us: that a good education resulting in a decent job can lift people out of poverty and off the welfare rolls. The proof lies in the 88% figure of their members who have graduated from college, left the welfare rolls and not returned.

IFSA was a cog in the coalition put together by the WRI to secure this legislation. In turn, that organization has joined our efforts to prevent the privatization of Social Security and Medicare. I established an endowed scholarship providing funds for one graduate a year to help further the WRI's advocacy program.

Another striking example of Hunter's participation in the life of the community is its Public Service Scholars program, made up mostly of women, which aims to develop leaders through training as interns with public officials. I was pleased to be able to contribute a scholarship to this program and to follow the careers of many of its participants who now hold positions in government.

As I mentioned earlier, in 1993, I was also invited to join the Board responsible for the college's Scholarship and Welfare Fund. Since I was eager to meet the students the fund assists, I was made a member of the Graduate Interview Committee, which decides on the applications for graduate grants.

It had been the customary procedure at the Fund, evolved through many years of experience, to make allocations to selected students without the expectation that they continue any further relationship with the Fund. When I asked the reason for this, one Board member expressed her belief that the recipients did not desire any additional contact. As proof, it was pointed out that some years before, several teas had been held to meet the recipients, but very few had expressed any interest in continuing the connection. Yet when the recipients were invited to the Fund's annual membership meeting, several of them expressed a keen interest in and appreciation of both the Fund and the college. An outreach committee was set up, which I was appointed to chair, to study the issue and return with a recommendation. We decided to work with the recipients of the Scholarship and Welfare Fund's Scholars' awards, because they had received four-year grants. We added to our committee a science professor, Ben Ortiz, himself a Scholars recipient, along with a number of other graduates who had received those grants.

After hearing our report, the Board decided to invite the 136 alumni scholarship recipients, the current selectees and a group of their favorite teachers, to a special celebration on April 14, 2004. The event was rated a huge success by all who attended it, and we have high hopes for the future success of this group.

Working with so many dedicated and effective young people at Hunter has both inspired me and provided me with a genuine sense of fulfillment. I am indebted, too, to the various alumni groups, particularly the Board members of the Scholarship and Welfare Fund and the extraordinary members of the faculty and staff. I have been able to balance the difficult years of the depression, during which I studied at Hunter, with a new feeling of hope and expectation, while at the same time repaying the college for the excellent education I received there. Through Meg Crahan, I met the chair of the History Department, Dr. Barbara Welter, and was invited to join the department members at their pleasant, candle-lit holiday parties. I also met the head of the Latin American and Caribbean Studies Program, Dr. Michael Turner, who was eager to share his knowledge. His mother, Jeanne Turner, was a graduate of one of the IFSA sessions.

In 1995, Dr. Crahan conducted a series of five seminars on "Human Rights in Latin America," climaxed by an international conference on "Human Rights in the 21st Century." The presenters at all of these events included eminent international human rights advocates and scholars. All the seminars were well attended and widely acclaimed, with many of those present rating them as among the best in which they had ever participated.

Sociology professors Ruth Sidel and Jan Poppendieck, who had been instrumental in founding Hunter's Center for the study of Family Policy, which had conceived WRI, were also helpful in insuring the success of one of IFSA's projects. They were part of the group that proposed an Oral History Project to interview the graduates of IFSA and were among those chosen to conduct the interviews. They are also, now, my warm personal friends.

I derived a great deal of satisfaction from planning the programs we put into effect with the various presidents of Hunter: the eloquent and witty Donna Shalala; the charming and erudite Paul LeClerc, currently heading the New York Public Library; and the innovative, community-minded David Caputo, who left after five years to preside over New York's Pace University. The latter encouraged me to become an inaugural member of the Library Fellows, a group of graduates who provide funds for the purchase of books needed by the college library. My gift is used to enrich the library's Latin-American section. That extended contribution also permitted me to name a room in the soon to be renovated Roosevelt House. I look forward to working with Hunter's current president, Jennifer Raab.

In 1994, New York State Governor Mario Cuomo bestowed upon me the "Senior of Distinction" award, which took the form of an award-winning sculpture executed by a student at New York University in a contest the college conducted for that purpose. When the director of public relations at Hunter College, Maria Terrone, issued a press release on the award, it resulted in an excellent, full-page story in the *New York Daily News*. At the same time, Bill Schleicher, then the assistant editor of the *Public Employee Press*, the publication of District Council 37 of AFSCME, was sent to interview me for that paper. As I reported earlier in my "Acknowledgments," this resulted in a special four-page supplement entitled "AFSCME's Untold Story," based largely on my organizing experiences in New York City's Department of Welfare and complete with pictures and with a caption that read: "Dorothy Epstein has been organizing for social justice since the 1930s. Today she trains seniors in modern political action techniques."

Schleicher also introduced me to the leaders of District Council 37's Women's Division and to Charles Ensley, president of Social Service Employees, Local 371, the organizational heir of the union to which I had originally belonged. In 1997, the Women's Division presented me with its first *Legacy Award*, and three years later, Local 371 conferred on me an honorary membership in the local.

In a sense, then, my organizational and academic life had come full circle—and a wonderful circle it has been!

Chapter 15
Celebrating 90

Slowly, surely and ineluctably, the years have rolled by. They have provided historic structure and memory's pegs on which to hang celebrations, changes in career and life style, and other major events. At 16 I marked my birthday and that of my best friend, Myrtle, by going on my first date, eating my first Chinese meal and seeing my first play; at 20 I graduated from college and started on my first real job; at 30 I gave birth to my son, Robert; at 40 and feeling almost middle-aged, I switched to a new career in the private sector; at 59 five male friends and I started our own business; at 60 I began to show signs that the number of years mattered when, because of my slower metabolism, my habit of doing business at meals resulted in increased weight, instead of the extra calories morphing, as before, into extra energy, and at 76 I retired from paid employment and returned to my first love, community work.

I had been rudely awakened to the fact that I was approaching ninety when Gertrude Groden died suddenly, leaving me, as the only volunteer of the Class of 1933, with the responsibility of planning our Seventieth Reunion. This was a significant one, as milestones go, ours was the next-to-last class to be recognized in reverse chronological order at the annual alumni luncheon.

Fortunately, our class historian, Tess Gloster, who had prepared our original milestone records, was still alive and able to supply much needed material. That, and the addition to our committee of two younger and experienced alumnae, Ursula Mahoney and Virginia Shields, enabled us to put together, almost seamlessly, an evocative introduction to the Class of 1933. Here is part of it:

Looking Backward: "Lives Well Lived"

The stringencies of nationwide depression gripped the class which entered college in 1929. We came to know, through personal experience, and saw in the world around us how fragile and uncertain life itself could be. Perhaps it was for this reason that we found such assurance in friendships and joy in the story of human search and achievement in every field we studied.

* * *

Courage and hope, fostered in college years and given voice by President Roosevelt as we graduated, brought us through the troubled times of waiting before we could find our place and work in the many spheres of endeavor we ultimately chose....We hope we have not been unworthy of the college that nurtured us—in Shakespeare's phrase, that we have proved "the mettle of our posture."

[We were able to use bios we had acquired when many more of the class members had been alive in order to supply information showing the large number of professions, arts, crafts and other working areas in which members of the class participated.]

Teaching, counseling and social work claimed most of us. To read our classmates' answers to past questionnaires is to hear voices of valor, intelligence and determination—and also of joy.

One class member wrote "not of fame throughout the wide world, but pleasure in a life 'well lived.'" Specifically, our list starts with non-profit groups, fighting for racial tolerance and better economic conditions; teaching—in elementary, high school and college; educational consultants; civil service, including counselors and supervisors; professional social workers; physicians; lawyers; librarians; secretaries; medical technologists; statisticians; retailing; a minister; a cartographer; a builder; a jewelry designer; a labor leader; a police official; a dietician, and an economist. Many graduates have written articles in their fields; one has edited, abstracted and researched publications in scientific fields; others have written books, including a biography of Edmund Burke, "The Politics of Welfare: A

New York City Experience," a book of poetry, children's books and "A Tool Kit for Advocacy." (I'm sure the reader will recognize the last-named of these).

*   *   *

There were pioneers among us who ventured at the beginning into conflicts the world struggles to resolve—Pauli Murray, one of the very few African-Americans in our class, who worked with Eleanor Roosevelt, fighting for racial justice and for women's acceptance in the fields of law and religious ministry; Felicia Spritzer, a pioneer for genuine equality for women in law enforcement; Eileen Egan, whose worldwide relief efforts, working with Dorothy Day and Mother Teresa, extended from Mexico to Poland, from India to China, and are recorded in her books and articles and reinforced by her place in international peace organizations; Blanche Bernstein, a trustee of Hunter College, was recognized for her work and the publication of her book, "The Politics of Welfare: A New York City Experience"; Dorothy Epstein strove for economic justice through union activities, helping build the largest public workers' union in the country and serving as its first woman New York State president; Sarah Lederman was widely recognized for her social work, and Lillian Cohen worked unceasingly to build a Jewish homeland.

THE CARTOON ON THE COVER of our reunion booklet was drawn by the noted *New Yorker* cartoonist, Roz Chast, daughter of a classmate. Her note accompanying the cartoon read simply: "Seventieth Reunion. Wow!" We included some poetry—old and new—and an additional feature provided by my son, a listing of important events that occurred in 1933, which was very much appreciated.

Deeply moving was a piece, "An Immigrant Comes to Hunter," by Alice Kalousdian Lanier, who had "arrived at Hunter a stranger in a new country," from Constantinople, and went on to reflect, "Am I imagining this, or do you share the feeling? At

Hunter we all mattered. When I said, 'I go to Hunter,' I held myself so tall that people thought me conceited. I went to a college that transformed a rootless immigrant girl into someone able to cope, to persist, to dream dreams. I went to Hunter College."

We also paid tribute to Gertrude Groden and mentioned those who had received school honors. We included a few photographs taken during our years at school. Everyone was pleased, and we had a 70th milestone book for our archives! We held our own special reception at which a dozen or so of us gathered to reminisce and enjoy a fabulous cheesecake baked by an IFSA graduate.

In June, 2003, I turned 90. One of my good friends at the Scholarship and Welfare Fund, Joan Lewis, hosted a small gathering at the Lotos Club. We lit a symbolic candle, toasted my advanced age, chatted interminably and had a thoroughly delightful time. Later that month, Bob and Marilyn brought together our close relatives and my dear friends going back to the trade union days for a wonderful lunch at a midtown restaurant. They were able to turn the event into an extraordinary tribute to advocacy, as one guest after another spoke extemporaneously about my IFSA experiences. My grandniece, Melinda Finkel, read a poem, *Aunt Dorothy*, which she had written especially for the occasion, and which read:

> Have you every struggled through the
> lush greens and tangles of a forest,
> About to freeze, stop breathing in the
> moist scent of fallen leaves –
> Only to realize you are traveling on footprints
> Someone else has packed down for you?
>
> When I pridefully tell someone about my Aunt Dorothy,
> I'm told, "It's in your blood"
> And I smile from the deepest of compliments
> As her lifetime of achievement starts to flood
> My mind and I rewind in time and start to list:

How she stood on her desk and took the risk
To start a union, attend Hunter's Seventieth Reunion,
Become the first woman president of
Synergy Vitamin Company,
How she founded the Institute for Senior Action....

And I stop reporting her socially con-
scious acts and enjoy the reaction,
As I recite a few of her awards from "Hometown Hero,"
To her induction into the National Women's Hall of Fame,
A day in New York City for her name,
And an additional wall of plaques to show
And more than a lifetime of her achieve-
ments starts to flood my mind
And I rewind in time and to the here and now
And I am amazed how her courage still runs past
Politics, across lines of religion, age and race.

Beauty, like the garden she grows on her balcony,
Shines the smile on her face, her
strength, only bolstered by a cane,
Continues to build foundations in the rain.

As her wisdom runs deep, water gathered in an
Ocean of a life well-lived, a globe well-traveled in taste
And her love as a mother, activist and friend,
Is large and constant, a river flowing beyond its end
Connected and cool, aware, funny
and as brilliant as a jewel.

I feel blessed to have her in my life
And want to thank her for the inspiration she gives me...
and to say "Happy Ninetieth Birthday!!!"

Then Bob spoke passionately, as did Rose Dobrof, founder of
the Brookdale Center on Aging, who has taught in every session
of IFSA but one; Meg Crahan, the first and current occupant
of the Dorothy Epstein Chair at Hunter College; Amy West

Poley, the inspiring director of JPAC; Bill Schleicher, editor of District Council 37, AFSCME's *Public Employee Press*, and Maureen Lane, co-director of the Hunter College's Welfare Rights Initiative and also an IFSA teacher. Each added a new dimension to the festivities.

A number of those present, including some who had played important roles in my life, refrained from participating in the speech-making for fear of extending the accolades indefinitely. They all came to me afterward to express their warm wishes. I spoke, but I don't remember what I said. The waiters, who hung around to listen, told my niece that they would vote for me if I ran for president. Unfortunately, there were no convention delegates around who could make that happen.

Then, at a JPAC meeting, candles were lit and another delicious cake consumed. This time, however, we honored everyone present over 90, and each of the 10 of us held a lighted candle to celebrate. The oldest was 94. As further recognition of their long service, they were all presented with copies of Granny D's book and Debra Bernhardt and Rachel Bernstein's remarkable work, *Ordinary People, Extraordinary Lives*. In my speech, which I remember, I paid tribute to the unending perseverance, hope and dedication of the JPAC members who were IFSA graduates and who brought so much to our advocacy efforts.

The year 2003 ended with separate events at which I was presented with the Hudson Guild's Elliott Community Service plaque (their highest award—10 years earlier, they had given me the Guild's Senior Award) and the Statewide Senior Action Council's Annual Harenberg Award for Senior Education. In the Fall, two university professors published *It's Never Too Late to Plant a Tree*, and I was one of 65 seniors chosen nationally to appear in the book. We were selected because each of us had begun, at a late age, an exciting new vocation.

And finally, just under the wire before I turned 91, early in June, 2004, we celebrated a decade of IFSA activities at a luncheon attended by 200 guests, at which we presented the Dorothy

Epstein IFSA Legacy Awards to Carl E. Haynes, president of Local 237 of the International Brotherhood of Teamsters, and to Juanita Doares, a graduate. Speaker after speaker (and we tried to keep the number to a minimum) spoke briefly, but eloquently, about the Institute's wonderful record of accomplishments. All 20 classes were represented, and a graduate of the first class and one from the most recent one spoke movingly about their experiences. One of them said she had become infused with so much energy that her neighbors no longer recognize her!

Ninety is certainly an age to remember—and to be remembered!

Chapter 16
Epilogue

I lay on my narrow, mechanized hospital bed, comfortable and secure, guarded on both sides by the button-raised side walls, my back relaxed as a result of the partially lifted bed frame and two pillows. In my half-dozing state, I was grateful for the quiet surrounding me. I had awakened that morning, Good Friday, 2005, with a long list of things to do, to find that I could not walk. I was both immobilized and panic-stricken. I called my son, Bob and cancelled my week's activities. The doctor's office was closed for the holiday, but Bob was able to reach him at the hospital. He brought me to the Beth Israel Hospital Emergency Room by taxi. I spent the rest of the day in a cubby hole, part of a long line of similar beds, waiting to learn what was wrong and whether or not they would keep me. For some reason, I wasn't hungry and was able to get through the day on the small breakfast I had had at home, supplemented by some water and apple juice.

From the little that they told me, I was able to gather that I had been bleeding heavily internally as a result of an infected duodenal ulcer. The bleeding had stopped, but there was considerable damage. It was decided that I should remain at the hospital in a private, carefully monitored room where my vital signs could be constantly checked. My son, Bob, was still with me and left only after he saw that I was safely ensconced.

It felt good, at about 10:15 p.m., to watch the pleasant nurse and her aide prepare my bed, check my gown, cover me and turn out the light. I was awakened several times during the night while the aide took more blood, checked my blood pressure, felt my pulse and once actually weighed me. When I opened my eyes after some sleep, I was able to discern, in the lowered light of the room, a young woman doctor, about 35 years old, staring intently at me. She seemed ill at ease. "I am your hospital doctor," she told me, "and I thought you should know everything we are doing. First, I must tell you that we're worried about you. You have lost so much blood, and your blood count is about one-third of what it should be, and that is dangerously low. We plan to give you two, more likely three, blood transfusions. We want to check every change that takes place in your body. We don't want to lose you."

For a moment, I was tempted to respond with such repartee as, "Nor do I want to lose you. I mean to stay around for a while." But somehow it just didn't seem right, and I remained silent. The doctor pressed my hand tightly and left.

I was a little angry because she had been so frank and yet I was not reacting strongly to her cautions. I was tired and a little apprehensive, but I just didn't feel like fighting—that is, until I thought of the mess we were facing in the world outside my hospital room: the danger of losing Social Security after 70 positive years; the imminent threat of cuts in Medicaid; the fact that one-half of the world's population lived on less than two dollars a day; the menace posed by global warming; our nation's disastrous foreign policy; and the morass in Iraq. This was not the time for me to go. There was too much to do.

ABOUT A MONTH AND A HALF LATER, on June 15, 2005, I attended the annual luncheon of *Jewish Currents*, a secular Jewish magazine, the brainchild of Morris U. Schappes. He was one of the City College professors who had lost their jobs in the early 1940s as a result of the activities of the Rapp-Coudert Committee, an early version of the McCarthy Committee. The magazine has existed through these many years because of the support of a loyal group of readers while other publications that were better financed have had to close down. Under the current editorship of Larry Bush, the magazine has been able to work out an arrangement whereby it has become the publication of the Workmen's Circle, a secular Jewish organization with a membership of some 16,000. Under the arrangement, Larry continues as editor, as do the members of the editorial board, enhanced by an equal number of Workmen's Circle representatives. As a result, *Jewish Currents* has been able to more than quintuple its circulation, and the luncheon I attended was the first held since this remarkable arrangement was consummated. The president of Workmen's Circle was on hand to greet us. What made the situation even more unusual was the fact that *Jewish Currents* had originally been launched by an organization established as a political counterbalance to the Workmen's Circle—the Jewish People's Fraternal Order (JPFO), part of the International Workers' Order (IWO), which later fell victim to the witch hunts of the McCarthy period.

I felt very fortunate to have had the opportunity to be present on this momentous occasion, particularly since the new editorial board of *Jewish Currents* had voted to publish a portion of this memoir in its Summer, 2005, issue. I could not help wondering what the reaction of my parents would have been to this strange confluence of events. Mama, I'm sure, would have welcomed it, but Papa?—is that sound I hear that of him turning over in his grave?

DOROTHY EPSTEIN

Index

About the Author

DOROTHY EPSTEIN grew up up in the immigrant communities of New York, entering the workforce during the worst part of the Depression. The child of activists herself, Dorothy had been loathe to follow in their overburdened, impoverished footsteps.

However, fate intervened, and Dorothy soon became radicalized. She spent most of her life working for the advancement of labor unions and human rights. In later years, Dorothy became a successful businesswoman in the vitamin industry. After "retirement," Dorothy went back to her organization work, this time devoting her attention to seniors, founding and consulting for the Institute for Senior Action (IFSA).

Dorothy Epstein died on May 25, 2006, at the age of 92.

Ben Yehuda Press presents
Jewish Women of the 20th Century

DOROTHY EPSTEIN. Growing up in the immigrant communities of New York, Dorothy Epstein entered the workforce during the worst part of the Depression. The child of activists herself, Dorothy had been loathe to follow in their overburdened, impoverished footsteps.

However, fate intervened, and Dorothy soon became radicalized and spent most of her life working for the advancement of labor unions and human rights. She died in 2006 at the age of 92.

A Song of Social Significance: Memoirs of an Activist by **Dorothy Epstein.** ISBN# 0-9769862-7-2

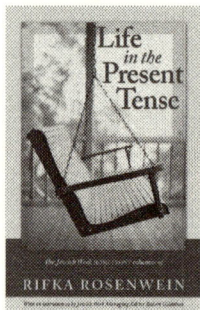

RIFKA ROSENWEIN. The daughter of Holocaust survivors, journalist Rifka Rosenwein chronicled her suburban, soccer-mom life in the back of *The Jewish Week* for seven years.

In 2001, Rifka's world was changed forever; first by the events of September 11th, and then, in a more personal blow, Rifka was diagnosed with cancer. She died in 2003 at the age of 42.

Even when she discusses her life as being lived on "cancer time," her columns are a death-defying celebration of life. Reading her work, you can see your own friends, your parents, your children, your co-workers, your spouse... and yourself.

Life in the Present Tense: Reflections on Faith and Family by Rifka Rosenwein. ISBN# 0-9789980-4-9

For more information, or to purchase these and other titles, visit your favorite bookstore or http://www.BenYehudaPress.com

Phone, fax, mail or e-mail to Ben Yehuda Press
430 Kensington Rd. Teaneck, NJ 07666
phone (201) 833-5145   *fax* (201) 917-1278
Credit card orders 800-809-3505
email orders@BenYehudaPress.com

Ben Yehuda Press presents
Jewish Women of the 20th Century

HANNE GOLDSCHMIDT. Nicolette Maleckar draws upon her experiences in post-war Berlin in telling the story of Hanne, a brave-hearted waif who must find a way to begin her life in the rubble of a shattered world. Hanne's story is a delightful rendering of the first blush of love in an impossible time. Her tale has been praised by West Virginia Public Radio for the "fairy-tale quality of the characters."

The Lilac Tree: An Enchanting Novel of Love in the Ruins of Berlin, 1945 by **Nicolette Maleckar.** ISBN 978-0976986225

BESSIE SAINER. Exiled to Siberia at age 12 for her brothers' anti-czarist activities, 25 loses her husband and baby girl to the ravages of civil war in revolutionary Russia. In America, she remains a "troublemaker," fighting Nazi hoodlums, going undergound to flee McCarthyite persecution, and nearly losing her beloved daughter amidst the civil rights struggles of the 1960s.

Narrating this novel at age 88, Bessie is still making trouble and still making jokes.

This is a profoundly optimistic novel about a remarkable heroine—a rebel, a lover, a mother, a grandmother, a nurse, a Jew, and an extraordinary human being. "It will grip you from beginning to end," says *Hadassah Magazine*. "A remarkable first novel," says *The Nation*.

Bessie: A Novel of Love and Revolution by **Lawrence Bush**
ISBN# 978-0978998035

For more information, or to purchase these and other titles, visit your favorite bookstore or http://www.BenYehudaPress.com

Phone, fax, mail or e-mail to Ben Yehuda Press
430 Kensington Rd. Teaneck, NJ 07666
phone (201) 833-5145 *fax* (201) 917-1278
Credit card orders 800-809-3505
email orders@BenYehudaPress.com

www.ingramcontent.com/pod-product-compliance
Lightning Source LLC
Chambersburg PA
CBHW021104090426
42738CB00006B/494